UPSIDE

May you always
find the Upside!
Best,
Allison
Blankenship

UPSIDE

HOW TO ZIG
WHEN LIFE ZAGS

29 Tips for Sustainable Success!

BONNIE MICHAELS
ALLISON BLANKENSHIP

Upside: How to Zig When Life Zags

Copyright © 2010 by Bonnie Michaels and Allison Blankenship

Published by Collage Books Inc.
4244 Corporate Square
Naples, Florida 34104
Email: info@collagebooks.com
Tel: 800-565-0922
Fax: 239-643-7883
www.collagebooks.com

ISBN: 978-0-938728-22-1

Library of Congress Control Number: 2010928034

Printed in the United States of America

10 9 8 7 6 5 4 3 2 1

Upside is available at special quantity discounts for bulk purchases for educational needs, promotions, premiums and fundraising. For details contact the publisher, Collage Books Inc.

TABLE OF CONTENTS

DEDICATION

We want to thank our dear Life Diva and friend, Patricia Varley, for her contributions to the book. Her spiritual strength and deep understanding of transformation and transition has guided our discussions on difficult topics. She is a rare, sensitive and knowledgeable person who helps individuals across the globe to make a better life. We are deeply indebted to her for her time and thoughtfulness.

~ Bonnie and Allison

BONNIE'S ACKNOWLEDGEMENTS

Writing this book was not a solitary process. So many individuals helped and encouraged us on our book development journey.

First and foremost I want to thank my loving husband, Michael Seef, who provided the background research to get the project off the ground. His daily support, encouragement and willingness to listen to ideas and read drafts are immensely appreciated. I can always count on him to provide an excellent explanation on a difficult topic and help me translate it for a reader.

A deep thank you to my dear friend, Rebecca Rolfes, the ultimate professional editor, for providing her wisdom, honesty and insights throughout our development. I am so grateful for the amount of time she spent reading, editing and questioning.

Hugs for my grandson, Tristan Michaels, who researched all the resources and saved us an enormous amount of time. His thoughtfulness and comments are a real contribution.

I wish to send many kudos to Dinah Rosenthal and Cindy Kulik who read through every page and made excellent comments. Thanks to Jeanne Berger's good questions and suggestions during our many walks, which were of enormous help.

I am so grateful to my friends and family in Naples for cheering me on, especially the Women in Transition group. They provided the backbone when things got tough. Hugs to Sue and Art

Bookbinder, Wendy and Jerry Richman, Saul and Janis Siegel, Doris and Alan Adlestein, Linda and Larry Hyde, Nancy and Jeff Kahn, Barbara and Steve Suden, and Myron Berger for their time, loving support and good thoughts.

My sincere appreciation to Jeff Hirsch, our publisher and advisor, who believed in the idea from the very start. His creativity, wisdom and humor made the process a real joy. Sandra Yeyati, our dear editor, provided excellent insights.

I appreciate all the stories of individuals who shared the good and bad times. They are the real heroes.

Finally, to my writing partner, Allison, who advanced the light side of our heavy subject. Her charm, good humor and creative approaches to a difficult topic made every day a delight.

~ Bonnie Michaels

ALLISON'S ACKNOWLEDGEMENTS

So many people were influential in the creation of this book. First and foremost, my deepest gratitude goes to my writing partner and life diva conspirator, Bonnie Michaels. Her passion for sustainable success is contagious, her spirit and energy endless, and her circle of influence life changing. Thank you for including and guiding me on such a marvelous journey.

My thanks also to my family and friends for their flexibility and inspiration: to Sandi Gornati, for pushing me "off the cliff"; Dr. Kimberly Ventus-Darks for teaching me to fly; and my sage and sounding board, Elizabeth Anderson. You are treasures in my life.

To Gary Greenfield, Mace Horoff, Rebecca Rolfes, Julie Morgenstern, Michael Seef and everyone who patiently coached, inspired or reviewed the manuscript. You probably never thought this day would arrive!

And finally, Jeff Hirsch and Sandra Yeyati of Collage Books who made this project a reality. Their humor, insight, integrity and adaptability made our work seem effortless. I stand in awe of their vision and achievements.

To everyone reading this book, we applaud you. The zags life throws you are merely upsides in disguise. Get ready to zig your way to success!

~ Allison Adams Blankenship

INTRODUCTION

MOVING WITH CHANGING TIMES

Most Americans have been affected by the zigs and zags of the economy and global change over the last few years. They have experienced dramatic changes that bristle with contradictions. The stock market boasted historic highs while employment rates plummeted. Internet startups crashed in a technology bubble, only to flourish again. Oil prices skyrocketed, dropped, and continue to confound the world. Turmoil in the banking and real estate sectors dramatically destabilized our economy. Against all odds, Americans elected this country's first minority president. These highs and lows have created an atmosphere of chaos and confusion. What used to be a sure thing is no longer; the rules are changing.

This book will help you set a course for the future as you navigate a continually shifting world. As your life moves into this uncharted territory, it is time to analyze past choices and plan ahead. Most important will be your ability to identify the **"UPSIDE,"** or positive opportunity in any given situation, for it is this ability that will empower you to harness the dynamic energy of change.

As professional work-life consultants, speakers and thought leaders, the authors have conducted workshops, focus groups and keynote presentations for years. Recently, we've heard several people say, "I'm just holding on until life gets back to normal." But we believe that things will not go back exactly to the way they used to be, and that we need new life skills and flexible success models that can withstand the test of a new time. Sharing our ideas, strategies and activities with workshop participants, we saw hope rekindle and energy soar as people began to build sustainable and happy lives.

To help them, we started with what we thought our own families might need. We began to craft a set of options to help individuals like you to move beyond the disappointment, despair and grief over the loss of a way of life and create a more stable and successful future, one that follows your authentic life path. We believe sustainable careers and lifestyles are possible. It will take changing your mind set and expectations, as well as your definition of success and happiness. It means changing the model of your work and personal life.

We can't make jobs magically appear, but we can provide strategies, resources and models for creating a satisfying life in a changing world economy. Ours is a holistic approach. It is not enough to recreate your professional life without reshaping your personal life as well; the reverse is also true. Most importantly, we aspire to help you explore career and personal life possibilities based on a long-term point of view.

Be assured that this is not a book crammed with economic equations. We are spouses, parents, grandparents, friends and lovers, just like you—not economists. It is important, however, to give you a comprehensive picture and to inspire, encourage and empower you, based upon our expertise in the fields of balance, change, problem solving, leadership and transition. Our country was founded on the pursuit of a better life, and our citizens have always seen the possibilities and pulled together in difficult times. It is said that we are at our best when challenged, and now is the time to summon our collective strength as a people. The spirit of America is hope; we encourage and support you in your journey.

THE PAST IS PAST

A crucial premise we are presenting is that our way of life will not return to the way it was. The American Dream, defined as "having it all," is in jeopardy. Many economists, futurists, researchers, environmentalists and social anthropologists claim that this downturn was inevitable. It has been suggested that this period is a time for the correction of a system that was based on speculation, overspending, overbuilding and record debt.

As we move forward, our economy must be based on responsible practices and sound principles—not flipping real estate, making loans that can't be repaid, over-the-top credit card spending, exaggerated consumerism and natural resource depletion. In a new, restructured economy, workers must plan for and live in a world of revised reality. This book addresses that challenge and provides solid solutions. Every chapter contains a series of stimulating and thought-provoking questions, personal stories and activities to guide the reader.

THE CHAPTERS

Many of you have experienced personal change and loss. **Chapter 1** offers the tools to accept these transitions and begin to move beyond them, understanding the need to create career and personal life models that will sustain you over the long term.

In **Chapter 2**, you take inventory of your current situation and analyze how and why you made decisions in the past. You will examine your underlying expectations of a successful life and identify factors that may be sabotaging your best efforts. You'll find tools to help you cope with the discomfort of living in an environment of constant change.

Elasticity and resilience are critical skills for long-term success. **Chapter 3** focuses on creating the mindset to adapt and develop a positive approach in times of change and uncertainty. Your goal is to rediscover purposeful meaning in your life and work. This process includes reclaiming your inner strength, passion and purpose.

Success and happiness is an elusive subject that is unique to each of us. In **Chapter 4**, you address the genesis of the American Dream and its significance for defining your own expectations and goals. This process lays the foundation for creating a sustainable and fulfilling life, based on the new reality.

Chapter 5 outlines the steps for long-term, satisfying work. You are challenged to use your creativity to uncover strengths and passions, and then apply them to find a fulfilling and sustainable career that is realistic in the changing world.

The relationship between money, happiness and success is a pivotal part of a changing work-life model. **Chapter 6** promotes a healthy attitude toward money, encouraging new ideas about your spending habits and uncovering your genuine identity beyond your financial self. The goal is for you to adapt and create new habits that integrate your career and personal life models, reflecting the reality of today's changing world.

Chapter 7 explains the importance of self-awareness as a source of focus and centering in times of chaos, in order to make good decisions about your career and personal life. Strengthening your inner life is an invaluable practice for dealing with a changing world. You will complete a series of exercises to assist with maintaining focus and commitment in the face of chaos or turmoil.

A holistic approach is key to create a successful and prosperous life that is sustainable. In **Chapter 8**, you are asked to look beyond your career model to all your lifestyle choices. The goal is to provide you with a set of options that reflects the new reality and allows you to thrive with less financial stress.

Chapter 9 addresses the isolation that many solopreneurs and individuals in transition experience. In this chapter, you identify how co-workers, friends and family may either support or derail your efforts to change, and how to remain resilient and focused while maintaining these relationships. Ideas are also provided for building a support community by reaching out through interest groups and online encouragement.

Chapter 10 provides the building blocks for holistic change by integrating the basic concepts provided throughout the book. The assessments, exercises and reflections completed from previous chapters assemble to provide you with a living, flexible whole-life plan.

As experts in the field, we recognize that altering the work-life paradigm isn't easy, but it is a must if we are all going to survive in this rapidly changing world. We encourage you to revisit the exercises often and utilize the resources listed in each chapter. You will need a journal or notebook to record your own thoughts, observations and exercise answers.

Ultimately, we are optimists at heart, and reiterate these facts: Our lives will be different in the future, as we join in the **UPSIDE** of change. Happiness and success can be ours with a life model that works in the new norm.

CHAPTER 1

WAKE UP TO A NEW REALITY

Toto, I don't think we're in Kansas anymore…
~ Dorothy, *The Wizard of Oz*

The Wizard of Oz, a groundbreaking film for its time, introduced a concept that is still true today: life as we know it has changed, and there's no going back. When Dorothy "landed" after a tornado ripped her farmhouse off its foundation, she cautiously opened the front door, having no idea what to expect on the other side. To her amazement, she discovered the breathtaking Technicolor beauty of Oz.

Because the tornado placed Dorothy into the unfamiliar landscape of Oz, she had little choice but to begin her quest. Amid fears and dangers lurking in the background, she and her new friends continued on the path, dealing with challenges as they occurred. They solved problems and explored new avenues while seeking (and attaining) their hearts' desires. Along the way, they gained wisdom and confidence.

Like Dorothy, many of you are experiencing an "Oz" moment. Your world has been knocked off its foundation and is in turmoil. You look back with longing at your seemingly predictable life before the tornado and feel a bit lost as you embark upon unfamiliar experiences.

These tornadoes are a natural part of life, although they may appear to be occurring more frequently in the 21st century. If you lost your life savings, a job, home or loved one, your life has been turned upside-down. You may find yourself holding your breath, waiting for things to return to normal. One fact is very clear as our economy emerges from a difficult time: what is "normal" has changed.

There is a new reality now—one that is important to understand if you are to create long-lasting, sustainable success. It is easy to focus on the negative aspects of this new reality: industries and jobs have disappeared, many businesses aren't hiring and getting small business loans can be difficult. Statistics on the economy change daily; it isn't necessary to depress you further by reiterating what you already know. And that's the key phrase: "what you already know."

Like Dorothy, you are on the threshold of a new life situation, your personal Oz. As you embark upon the unfamiliar terrain ahead, we will help you find the upside of every downside. You will learn to release what you already know, uncover the positive aspects of your new reality and embrace its new opportunities and beginnings.

The goal is to create sustainable success—a satisfying way of life that is achievable, manageable and ongoing. We'll give you the building blocks to unlock the upside of every situation and maintain long-term stability amidst ever-changing situations and opportunities.

In this book, you will encounter 29 tips for finding the upside of every situation. We begin with the number-one skill you will need to thrive and create long-lasting success.

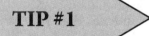
TIP #1

THE NOT-KNOWN IS THE NEW NORM

What does "not-known" mean and how is that different from "unknown"? The not-known, as we define it, includes events that cannot be anticipated, so they are not yet known to you and in most cases, not yet created or invented. The unknown, on the other hand, is elusive and mysterious, with the implication that you may never know its outcome or answer. The not-known is waiting to happen, while the unknown remains hidden and incomprehensible.

The 2008 presidential campaign is an example of a not-known becoming known. Many political experts predicted that this country would elect its first female president, Senator Hillary Clinton. Then a not-known candidate emerged: Senator Barack Obama. As Obama became a known entity, the United States elected its first African-American president, instead of a female. This situation highlights the not-known process; if political experts had suggested that the country would elect a black president two to three years prior to the race, no one would have believed it.

Not-knowns are works in progress, developing opportunities and emerging factors that impact your life. Computers, cell phones and ATMs were all not-knowns at some point. Conversely, unknowns may never be confirmed or determined. A common unknown many people wonder about is the question of life after death. There is an important different between these two concepts. Unknowns may never be discovered. Not-knowns, as we define them, will eventually be revealed.

The new reality of the next decade is that the not-known is a daily certainty. Life is changing so quickly that you cannot possibly know all of the opportunities that exist or are being created, even as you read this. Futurist Faith Popcorn predicted that during the first five years of the new millennium (2000 to 2004) our society would undergo 50 years worth of change, and that the following five years (2005-2009) would encompass 100 years of change.

The U.S. Department of Labor estimates that today's college graduate will have eight different careers—not jobs—in their lifetime. Our lives are changing at warp speed; we are surrounded by not-knowns. Many of the reliable constants or "rules" in our lives are changing. Here are just a few examples that you may be experiencing:

Value	Old Rule	New Rule
Loyalty	Find a good company, do a good job, and they'll take care of you for the rest of your career.	Find a network of people with whom you are compatible and follow their course. Develop your brand and distinguish your abilities.
Compliance	Maintain the status quo, don't rock the boat and stick with the traditional approach.	Creativity rules. What worked six months ago may not be applicable today. Think outside the box.
Prosperity	Anyone can achieve the dream, because resources and opportunities are endless.	Prosperity is a mindset related to overall happiness, not money or material gain. Develop greater consciousness about resource consumption.
Productivity	Work 40 hours a week with a little overtime and stick to the schedule for 25 years.	Do whatever it takes to get the job done. 40 hours is an ideal. Minimize overtime expenses.
Balance	An annual vacation and a few holidays are sufficient to replenish your energy.	Balance is a continual ritual. Shorter, more frequent vacations are needed.
Longevity	Pick a career and stick with it for life, earning raises, promotions and a guaranteed pension.	Don't get comfortable in one position for too long. Leadership and ownership change frequently. Reinvent your strengths and talents to fit available opportunities.

The upside is that you can create new rules for yourself that will allow you to harness the power of change. This is a good time to examine your goals and success models and adapt them to new circumstances.

> *By embracing the mystery of uncertainty, we will find its own forms of beauty and energy and coherence—and we will discover in ourselves the ironic capacity to be renewed and even transformed by the shock of insecurity.*
>
> ~ David Shi

According to economic predictions, the new norm will be one of lowered financial expectations, reduced consumerism and concurrently shrinking debt, with more savings. Don't be surprised if things don't go back to the days of easy money, high-end consuming and soaring wages. As a result of the stock market crash and Great Depression of the 1930s, people changed their consumption and debt behaviors for at least a generation. Likewise, the great recession you are currently experiencing will have its own momentous impact. If handled skillfully, this experience can lead to success.

Many experts suggest that this economic downturn is an overdue correction. It is an excellent time for our government to alter its economic and regulatory policies, and for individuals to change old habits. Although past goals and dreams may be affected, a correction can lead to more realistic aspirations.

The traditional American Dream, as defined in the past, probably can't be achieved in the new norm. North America is beginning the long process of rebuilding and correcting its economy and industries. Since World War II, the United States has historically experienced cyclical trends of ups and downs, with intermittent recessions. This economic rollercoaster ride is a normal part of the country's development, so get ready for more ups and downs. You will need to readjust and make corrections. The upside is that it could improve your way of life.

> *Our national policies have distorted economic activity away from savings and investment in industry and toward consumer consumption, housing and finance.*
>
> ~ Shelia Blair, FDIC chair

As old ways of working and living fade away in the new norm, alternative ones take their place. How you approach these changes and new events to rebuild the American Dream can determine your success. Think about what your personal expectation of the Dream includes for you. Financial security? Time with loved ones? A comfortable place to live? Travel? Everyone has their own unique, personal dream.

Sometimes, dreams center around the concept of acquiring things rather than experiencing moments. For instance, when buying a house, most of us tend to focus on the "bells and whistles" versus ways we can live, play and create memories in it as a home. We often judge our dreams by visible, tangible characteristics. The new norm recreates this experience; by choosing a smaller home, you now have more time to spend with loved ones, instead of taking care of a larger property.

The downside of acquiring is that your energy is consumed by working to support an unsustainable lifestyle. As a result, you are stressed, exhausted and struggle to enjoy the benefits of your hard work. Have you sacrificed important values such as time for self, family and community in pursuit of these dreams? Did you head down the path of unnecessary consumption without even thinking about it, losing yourself in the process? Whether you have or not, this time of chaos is an opportunity to evaluate your career and personal life choices and re-examine your core beliefs.

CLARIFY YOUR CORE VALUES

Core values and beliefs are traits or qualities we consider worthwhile; they represent an individual's highest priorities and deeply held, driving forces. Core values affect your success.

What are some of the core values or beliefs with which you live your life? Friendship, respect for others, life balance and spiritual beliefs are all examples of core values. As you explore the suggestions and ideas in this book, core values will play an important role, so start a list of important values and beliefs that matter to you. Your list may take a while to put together, as most of these beliefs are so ingrained into your personality that it may be difficult to discern or recognize them at first. You'll have many opportunities to define and use these concepts throughout the book.

SUSAN'S EXPERIENCE: CLARIFYING PERSONAL CORE BELIEFS

After several years abroad, living and working in multiple countries, Susan returned to the U.S. with a notable difference in her personal values. One of her observations was that the American Dream of "having it all" came at the expense of giving up time for self, family and friends. She noticed that the pressure of working long hours to keep pace with the American way of life had a price. While living and working abroad, Susan was able to assume the pace and traditions of the local culture and feel relaxed about it.

Upon returning, it was difficult for her to adjust to the lack of time for simple things like eating lunch with a friend versus at her desk in the office; or having lengthy conversations about world issues instead of watching the clock. According to Susan, the American way of life has its advantages in terms of comforts and opportunities, but sometimes sacrifices the simple joy of daily life without pressure or guilt. Susan's experiences reinforced her core belief that it's okay to take the time to enjoy meaningful activities despite opposing cultural norms.

Now it's your turn. Think about your current definition of being successful or living your dreams, and jot down your thoughts about what that means to you.

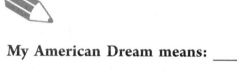

My American Dream means: _____

_____

_____

_____

_____

_____

As you review your notes about living your dream, are you confident that it is still achievable or possible? No one could predict the changes that are taking place globally; they are unprecedented. You are probably feeling disoriented, uncertain and pulled in a million different directions. Rest assured that you are not alone in your concerns about the future. Embracing the power of the new norm and the not-known allows you to move beyond the anxiety and employ new ways of working and living. To be successful, new skills, attitudes and models are required to lead fulfilling work and personal lives.

The journey upon which you are embarking is not speedy. There are no quick answers or fast fixes to make. This book outlines a holistic approach that combines mind, heart and soul to create a sustainable career and personal life. The upside is that this approach can incorporate many of your current skills; the challenge is that it does so in a way that requires a complete paradigm change. In other words, the assumptions, concepts, values and practices that shape your way of viewing reality are going to shift.

> *You never change things by fighting the existing reality. To change something, build a NEW model that makes the existing model obsolete.*
> ~ R. Buckminster Fuller

Americans have always risen to the challenges presented to them. You can draw comfort and inspiration from visionaries who have been on the forefront of new inventions, technology, jobs and ways of living, such as Thomas Friedman, Robert Reich, Juliet Schor, Bill Gates and Joseph Stiglitz. Like these futurists who explored new concepts, you too have the freedom to create a new model, based upon your core values and new expectations for success. The options and resources presented in this book will help you to navigate a new direction in these chaotic times.

In the Hopi Indian tradition, there are predictions about a time when things fall apart in order for things to come together again. If your life feels like it is falling apart, now is the time to plan for *true* happiness in your work and personal life. It is an opportunity to redesign and explore ways to create a sustainable life.

ABANDON THE MYTH OF JOB SECURITY

There was a time when the American worker could expect to work at one job until retirement and be rewarded with the famous gold watch. People stayed put, regardless of whether that was productive for either the employee or the company. Over time, loyalty and commitment were mistaken for a guarantee of job security. People wrongly believed that working hard would protect them from downsizing and termination, but the last 30 years have dismantled these beliefs. Record unemployment and an unpredictable economy have created a sense of isolation and uncertainty, along with a feeling of sentimental bereavement for the past.

If you are employed, your job longevity is uncertain in the not-known. The new norm is moving away from jobs and positions to sustainable skills and talents that are marketable, transferable commodities. The upside involves shifting your focus from finding job security to finding work that showcases your strengths and abilities in a constantly changing workplace.

Pamela Mitchell, founder of The Reinvention Institute, predicts, "Your ability to change directions is your new job security. Even if you haven't felt the recession's impact yet, the more proactive you are, the better protected you'll be if the other shoe drops." The choices you make now will either open or close doors for you in the future. This book helps open your eyes to recognize and act upon these options.

The new norm can release you from defining yourself through a job. When people inquire about what you do, it's not uncommon to state your job title. If you've been in a position or industry for a long time, you may feel a loss of identity without it. This is an occasion to redefine yourself. It is a time of rebirth for your self, your country and your world.

Don't worry if you feel lost during this chaos. Dark times and disappointments can often engender great creativity and opportunity. You are a catalyst for the rebirth to occur. The upside is achieved by exploring new pathways to happiness and a security that comes from within, not from outside. It is time to reestablish your true nature by becoming self-sufficient, resilient and resourceful.

THE UPSIDE OF THE DOWNTURN

Consider the fact that an economic downturn is not all bad. Less business activity results in fewer workplace accidents and less pollution. With added personal freedom and time, some unemployed individuals choose to smoke less, exercise more and make healthier food choices. They have time for family and friends. As house prices fall, first-time homebuyers and low-income families benefit. Consumers enjoy lower prices too, as the demand for goods and services dwindles. Less commuting and a growing bias against larger, less efficient vehicles lowers the consumption of oil and gasoline, further reducing costs.

> *When you lose a job it is like dying but out of death comes new life. You have to go through the dark night of the soul.*
> ~ Mary Lynn Pulley,
> *Losing Your Job—Reclaiming Your Soul*

The recession is creating opportunities to correct an imbalanced economy. The United States economy has moved away from manufacturing and industry, toward service-oriented employment, relying heavily on the technology and healthcare sectors. This is a chance to regain a better balance between manufacturing and service. How does this affect you? In order to sustain the future growth of our gross domestic product (GDP), the workforce must innovate, become more flexible, efficient and possibly sustain wage reductions. Your ability to navigate well through these corrections is a key component of your success.

EARTH MATTERS – THE ROLE OF NATURAL RESOURCES

Your success in the future depends, in part, upon the availability of natural resources. We are already experiencing amplified storm seasons and increasingly severe winters. Other effects – such as global climate change – are not yet completely understood. As you plan ahead, it is important to identify both short-term and

> *People are using about a third more of Earth's capacity than is available, undermining the resilience of the very ecosystems on which humanity depends.*
> ~ Erik Assadourian

long-term environmental changes, and to be aware of both local and global conditions. Short-term, local concerns include periodic droughts or extreme weather patterns; long-term issues include global climate change, as well as the depletion of oil, water, and forests. Becoming aware and adjusting your lifestyle to changing conditions is fundamental to your ability to sustain a personal life.

As you connect the dots in this chapter, there is a pattern emerging for you; the new norm requires ideas and strategies you may not have tried in the past. Keep in mind that in *The Wizard of Oz*, the journey for Dorothy and Toto was not only frightening and frustrating, but also exhilarating and enlightening. In the end, Dorothy and Toto found their way back home with more confidence and a greater appreciation of their loved ones.

Unlike Dorothy's, your journey is holistic, multi-dimensional and encompasses economic and environmental awareness, as well as a creative repurposing of your life. This book will give you the tools and guide you through the strategies needed to get back on solid ground.

REMINDERS:

- **The not-known is the new norm.**

- **The rules have changed. Write your own.**

- **Take advantage of this time of correction to adjust your own life.**

- **Clarify your core values to determine what is most important to you.**

- **Revisit your American Dream.**

- **Abandon the myth of job security.**

- **Look for the upside of the downside.**

CHAPTER 2

GET OUT OF
THE RABBIT HOLE

*Well, after such a fall as this, I shall think nothing
of tumbling down stairs!*

~ Alice in Wonderland

In Lewis Carroll's classic, *Alice in Wonderland*, Alice follows the white rabbit down a rabbit hole into a fantasy world. Do you ever feel that the chaos in your life has taken you down such a rabbit hole, shattering your illusions of comfort and safety? Have the doors of opportunity been locked to you? Are you uncertain about how to resolve your career or personal life issues? Are the keys too heavy to lift and the way out blocked or confusing?

Now is the time to assess your new reality and create a plan for sustainable, ongoing success. To unlock the doors, you need curiosity, flexibility and creativity, just like Alice. Every effective solution begins with a strong assessment of the situation. Your life is no different. The upside of being stuck is learning from your past.

LOOK BACK TO PLAN AHEAD

The following exercise is an excellent information-gathering tool that asks you to look back at your past actions, including career and personal decisions. This may help you unlock future opportunities. When you look into choices and patterns from your past, you can see why you do the things you do, learn how you make decisions and better understand yourself. With this knowledge, you can then consciously move forward with new decisions and choices.

Use the following worksheets to diagram your career and personal life decisions. Be brutally honest with your answers, because this exercise will give you important insights. It may take several days to reflect upon your past, so take your time.

CAREER TIMELINE EXERCISE

Date	Job description	Reason you took job

CAREER TIMELINE EXAMPLE

Date	Job description	Reason you took job
1982	Montessori teacher	Stable job. As a single parent, steady income needed. Interesting area; opportunities for growth and using skills.
1992	Corporate trainer	Opportunity for advancement, health care, growth, & good income.

As you review the timeline of your professional past, what stands out? Did you move from job to job as part of a sustainable, strategic course, or were the moves based more on timing and opportunity? Consider the following questions to clarify your professional past:

1. What factors influenced your career? For example, were you attracted to opportunities based upon financial gain, personal interests or something else? _____

   _____

   _____

2. Which core values or models were you able to follow or demonstrate in these positions or relationships? For example, were you able to act as a mentor and express strong personal development skills? Did you gravitate to team-based efforts and shared goals? Think about the personal beliefs and values each job or position allowed you to experience. _____

   _____

   _____

   _____

3. Which career decisions were based upon your knowledge of future business trends or needs? For example, did you predict that customer service or technical support jobs

would be outsourced overseas? If so, how did you prepare
for that? _____

_____

_____

4. How did you research each of these jobs beforehand?

_____

_____

_____

5. Were career choices based upon your expertise, passion
    for the job, geographical location, financial rewards or
    something else? Which of these motivators appears most
    frequently in your professional history? Do you see any
    patterns? _____

_____

_____

6. What elements have changed in your job or industry and
    what is not working for you now?_____

_____

_____

_____

7. What can you learn from your professional past that will
    help you make more sustainable decisions? _____

_____

_____

_____

8. List the core values you will now use to redefine your career
    and personal life so that they are more sustainable.

_____

_____

_____

PERSONAL LIFE TIMELINE EXERCISE

Date	Personal life decision	Reason you made decision

PERSONAL LIFE TIMELINE EXAMPLE

Date	Job description	Reason you took job
1994	Moved to Los Angeles	Husband's career opportunity.
1998	Purchased home	Investment. Good community to raise a family.
2005	Sold home. Purchased condo	Simplify lifestyle and expenses. Free up cash for retirement investing.

Your past reveals motivators, patterns and choices. Review your personal life timeline to clarify factors that have led you to where you are now.

1. Which decisions contributed to your success and happiness? Describe what made the difference for you.

   _____

   _____

   _____

   _____

2. Can you identify a pattern of factors or theme that influenced your personal life choices? For example, are you attracted to relationships where you can provide love and support, or do you prefer to be supported?_____

_____

_____

_____

3. How have your core values shaped your choices and/or direction? Who provided strong role models for these values? Where and how are you able to demonstrate them to others? _____

_____

_____

_____

4. How have global trends impacted your relationships? For example, if friends and family have lost their jobs or been outsourced, how has that impacted your feelings or relationship? _____

_____

_____

_____

5. Which decisions were made without analyzing the future trends for investments, real estate and natural resources? How did this affect your daily relationships?_____

_____

_____

_____

6. What elements have changed in your personal life, and what is not working for you now?_____

_____

_____

7. What factors beyond your control have impacted your choices? For example, divorce or death of a loved one.

_____

_____

8. What have you learned about your past personal choices that will contribute to better planning in the future?

_____

_____

RACHEL'S STORY

Several years ago, Rachel had the opportunity to start her own business. She resisted for a long time; self-employment was never a personal goal. Rachel preferred the structure of working for organizations and corporations, where it was comfortable and secure. But when she married and inherited small children, she changed the way she viewed her personal and professional lives. Attempting to give 100 percent to both relationships was exhausting, and she knew something had to give.

Rachel completed the timeline exercises and was stunned at what they revealed. She liked to think of herself as a proactive person, but the career timeline showed her that she was more passive, waiting for opportunities to come along instead of creating them. On numerous occasions, she allowed her employer to place her in jobs that she didn't like, because she wanted to be appreciated for being a team player. On the inside, she felt like a victim who had no control over what fate the corporation decided for her.

Understanding how she arrived at that realization was an eye-opener. It gave her the courage to start her own training and motivational speaking business. While the start-up was difficult, she now enjoys freedom and creativity that was never present in past jobs. As her own boss, she released the victim mentality, accepted full responsibility for her success and learned to make decisions that enhanced her career goals and personal sustainability.

Now that you've assessed where you are and understand the patterns and choices of your life, it's time to move forward with a new plan. The fact that you are reading this book is a sign that you are intellectually preparing for the next step. If you are like most people, however, you may find this is not as easy as anticipated. That's mostly due to your comfort zones.

TIP #5

BUST YOUR COMFORT ZONE BARRIERS

Comfort zones are comprised of information and ideas you accept as true and skills you believe you possess. As you read in Rachel's story, she didn't want to start a new business because that behavior was outside her personal comfort zone. She believed that self-employment would take time away from her family. Rachel discovered, however, that the benefits of moving beyond her limited comfort zone far outweighed the costs. She learned to flex and grow her comfort zone to include new professional experiences.

Here's the great news about your comfort zones: they can only get bigger. Alice's risk-taking sent her into the not-known territory of the rabbit hole, which was quite distressing, but she used her curiosity and problem-solving skills to unlock doors. This success increased her confidence and expanded her comfort zone. What a great upside to stress.

As opposed to Alice, who chose to follow the rabbit, you may have lost a job, financial security or life partner due to circumstances beyond your control. You did not choose to move out of your comfort zone. Still, the road to success is the same. As discussed in Chapter 1, your future depends on the ability to feel comfortable with the not-known. It is time to flex and stretch your existing comfort zones and bust through any barriers holding you back. By learning to harness your resilience, creativity and problem-solving skills, you can create long-lasting, sustainable success, identifying exciting new opportunities along the way.

Confronting the not-known and moving out of your comfort zone are not pleasant, but your ability to accept the new reality is critical to your survival. When you convert your resistance into energy and dig deep inside for strength, you will uncover new career and personal life possibilities. Operating out of your comfort zone can strengthen your core values and analytical skills.

When you accept the discomfort of new experiences, you can begin to use it to your advantage. Feelings of uncertainty may force you to clarify what is really important. Once you are focused, you can move to the next stage and use your creativity to strategize on subsequent steps for a new career and personal life. If you have experienced many losses, acknowledge that you have little to lose by trying new ways of working and living.

BETTY'S STORY

Betty and her husband Michael took a one-year sabbatical to travel around the world, exchanging their time and talents for room and board. They stretched their comfort zones daily, arriving in foreign countries without the usual comforts of a familiar language, daily life structure, home, job and friends or family. Their goal was to uncover new meaning and possibilities for their work and personal lives.

The trip was launched with open-ended airline tickets and one suitcase apiece. The couple made no hotel reservations beyond the first week and started in Spain, with plans to study and volunteer. Their yearlong travels took them to Japan, India, Israel, Germany and Australia. The journey proved to be a life-changing event as they maneuvered through intense problem-solving situations. They learned to communicate in several languages and travel safely, collected meaningful experiences and interacted with individuals from other cultures.

The upside of this trip was a new appreciation of the good life they enjoyed in the United States. They also strengthened their creative problem-solving skills, increased their flexibility and open-mindedness and learned about frugal financial management. The experience helped them clarify their priorities, both personal and professional. Many of the lessons and skills they obtained on their trip have helped them deal with today's new reality. The not-known became their friend; they welcomed the chance to try new things and were awakened to new ways of living and working.

DEFINING YOUR COMFORT ZONES

As you begin to stretch yourself in this new process, pay attention to the origin of your discomfort. Is this experience challenging a belief you hold or is it physically uncomfortable? Does it make your palms sweat? Do you feel unsafe? These reactions are normal and signal which part of your comfort zone is actually growing and which areas exhibit limiting beliefs or barriers.

Your comfort zone can be broken down into multiple areas of experience: physical, emotional, spiritual, financial and intellectual. The physical zone is easy to detect as your body sends you real symptoms, via hormonal or muscular reactions. Think about the physical discomfort of starting a new exercise program; your body responds with lactic acid to the workout, which results in muscle cramps or soreness. Once your body becomes conditioned, the aches disappear as

> *Things do not change; we change.*
> ~ Henry David Thoreau

the muscles recognize the exercise program. The same is true with your other zones: the more you encounter new emotional experiences, the easier it is to recognize and respond the next time you encounter a similar situation.

Once you identify the specific zone or basis for your discomfort, it is much easier to flex and readjust that zone. Consider the outcome if you do not continue to grow and become stagnant: burnout, depression, boredom and frustration are all common indicators of a comfort zone in need of attention or stimulation.

Your journey into the new norm of the not-known is certain to challenge your existing levels of comfort. Sweaty palms are often a sign that you are on the right track; fear may be a sign that you are in the presence of something to learn. Rather than avoiding them, you may want to make a decision that causes your palms to sweat or engenders a bit of fear, just to keep you energized and evolving. Keep in mind that taking risk without knowledge can lead to disaster, so be certain to make well-researched, calculated decisions on a weekly to monthly basis that bust your comfort zone barriers.

MAKE LOSS AND CHANGE A SPRINGBOARD FOR SUCCESS

As devastating as your losses may be, they can still have positive benefit if you allow them to act as a springboard for success. Have you ever considered that an upside of loss is that it creates space for something new? Life in the new norm is about change. To be successful during great change, you must commit to personal and professional growth. With that in mind, imagine yourself using the empty space that loss or change created and rebuilding your life with greater energy, ideas, wisdom and knowledge.

In the timeline exercise, you learned about yourself and your motivations for decision-making. You are now ready to springboard into new life choices. Because there is a natural inclination to have some fear about moving into the unknown, you may be thinking that you don't want to make mistakes that could set you back again.

In Chapter 3, we will explore the topics of fear and loss in depth. It is important to point them out here because they are so crucial to your growth and development in the future. Fear is a test of our will, which we must overcome in order to succeed. When we can acknowledge it and move beyond it, we are on the right path. Ask yourself what is the worst thing that can happen if you take a step in a direction that seems fearful. Step by step you can remove some obstacles. Take a moment to reflect on these inspirational thoughts:

Fear is moving toward the truth.

~ Pema Chodron, *Comfortable with Uncertainty*

With every ending there is also a beginning. Pay attention to
and foster what you love, not what you fear.

~ Robin Sheerer, career consultant

TIP #7

ELIMINATE EXPECTATION AND ENTITLEMENT

Feeling that you are entitled to a certain way of life, or expecting it to turn out a certain way, could be holding you back from success and happiness. Almost everyone harbors a sense of entitlement somewhere in their life, where they believe that they *deserve* a particular reward or benefit. Many of us were raised by parents who expected us to get an education, find a great job, buy a house and start a family. While that may have been possible for your parents, it set the bar for unrealistic expectations and feelings of entitlement for you today. For example, do you believe that your boss should notice how hard you work? Do you ever feel that other people do not appreciate you as much as they should? Have you ever thought that someone else gets all the lucky breaks? These are all signs of entitlement.

Believing that you are entitled to a certain lifestyle is a roadblock to your success and happiness. When we believe that we have a right to claim something, we are not taking responsibility for our own actions and choices.

Identify areas in which you feel entitled. Could they be getting in the way of moving forward? Are you attached to the idea that you should get what you want? What are your entitlement hooks: pleasure, gain, praise, fame, money? Or, are you feeling angry or bitter about career, financial or lifestyle losses?

With all of the changes and losses occurring in your life, it's important to determine if you are angry because you expected a different outcome. Do you feel that these events are fair or within your control? If you can detect the source of your entitlement beliefs, the upside is that it will be easier to move ahead on your journey to sustainable success. Holding on to what life should have been will make dealing with the not-known more difficult.

The following exercise is designed to help you identify where entitlement attitudes come into play. Think about each statement thoroughly and be brutally honest.

"I DESERVE" ACTIVITY

Circle a number from one to seven that best expresses your feeling about the statement.

1	2	3	4	5	6	7
Strongly Disagree						Strongly Agree

Answer in terms of how you really feel, not how you think you should feel.

_____ 1. I deserve a good-paying job because of my abilities.

_____ 2. I deserve to be treated fairly.

_____ 3. I deserve respect from others.

_____ 4. I deserve to be treated the way I treat others.

_____ 5. I deserve recognition for my accomplishments.

_____ 6. I deserve a good life.

_____ 7. I am entitled to "life, liberty and the pursuit of happiness."

_____ 8. I deserve a break from all my financial losses.

_____ **Total score**

SCORING

Add the numbers and divide that total by eight. If you scored 1-2, you are probably frustrated, but maintaining a good outlook. If you scored 3-4, you are battling to hold your grip and may feel occasional outbursts of anger. A score of 5-7 indicates that you need to readjust your expectations to alleviate some of the pressure or anger you feel.

Are you surprised by your score? On the surface, these statements seem to be reasonable expectations, but given the new norm of the not-known, you can't depend on past logical outcomes. Expecting these behaviors or outcomes can sabotage your plans to create more sustainable success. As you look over your list, ask yourself how these entitlements may prevent you from moving ahead.

What did you learn from this exercise? How much are you expecting from others and situations? Can you let these expectations go and accept that there are no guarantees in this world? If you can, you'll enjoy the upside of moving forward in a more proactive and positive way.

TIP #8

ATTITUDE = OUTCOMES

The attitude with which you address challenges and opportunities affects their outcomes. This doesn't suggest that you blindly accept your losses; it is important to properly grieve and process these events in your life. Only then can you examine them in light of current realities and global economics. Setbacks are part of life, but in light of the new norm, there may be more setbacks than you anticipated. Your goal is to see the upside when unexpected problems occur.

How do you acquire the discipline to prevent or redirect a bad attitude? The first step is to be aware that it is happening. By being conscious of your attitudes and thoughts, you stay in the present moment, rather than dwelling on the past or worrying about the future.

USING AN ATTITUDE OF GRATITUDE
TO COMBAT NEGATIVITY

One of the most powerful attitude adjusters is to give thanks for all aspects of your life—the good, the bad and the ugly. Begin with the easier task of expressing gratitude for the good things in your life, like the support of loved ones, newfound freedom or fulfilling work. Continue by expressing gratitude for the not-so-happy circumstances, which is an extremely powerful way to develop a positive outlook regardless of your situation. You can't be depressed if you are feeling thankful.

There are always extreme situations, such as the loss of a loved one or tremendous natural disaster, that make this concept difficult to bear or embrace. However, it can be a powerful upside to recognize grace during difficult times. Being grateful for all life experiences will help you rebuild your life and stabilize personal chaos. You can conquer your fears by focusing on the positive aspects of your life and believing that you will find answers.

List all the people, relationships and aspects of your life for which you are grateful. _____

_____

_____

_____

Barbara and Charlie's story

Barbara and her husband Charlie worked very hard at their careers in theater and music. In planning for retirement, they put their money in investments they believed to be safe. Unfortunately, in these changing times, they lost the majority of their savings. The loss was devastating. In addition to their own financial loss, their divorced daughter could not make mortgage payments on her home. All in all, the couple was torn emotionally and financially.

The duo had been well-known for their ability to turn things around and focus on the positive. In the past, when setbacks occurred they rarely allowed negativity to enter into the picture. However, as older adults, they were frightened and rightfully concerned about their financial future.

When it became apparent that retirement was no longer on their horizon, Barbara and Charlie each took a deep breath and confronted their fears by going back to work. They also focused on the most positive aspects in their lives, their children and grandchildren, who brought them great joy. Even with their financial crisis, they made a commitment to help their daughter temporarily with her mortgage payments. By moving their attention away from their own issues and feeling grateful for their ability to help others, the couple was able to move from a place of distress to action.

TIP #9

PRACTICE RESILIENCE

To counter the chaos in your life, there is one characteristic you might have forgotten: resilience, the ability to endure and thrive.

Resilience can pull you out of chaos toward clarity. You may not think that you have resilience, but it is deep inside your human nature. Think about a circumstance that was forced or painful for you. At what point did you decide you were tired of being unhappy in that situation? When did you determine that you wanted and/or needed something different in your life? That was you, being resilient.

The upside of reflecting upon past experiences is that you can validate your previous practice of resilience. Consciously or unconsciously, you've called upon that resilience to get back on your feet. It is helpful to look at your present situation as just another setback on your life's journey. For some individuals, the setbacks may be more severe than ever before—monetary loss, foreclosures or the death of a loved one. No matter the situation, tapping into your inner strength and resilience and combining it with knowledge gained from past experiences is a powerful tool to move you forward and create a sustainable life.

Tracey's story

Early in Tracey's advertising and television production career, it was clear that her values and ideals did not match industry standards. Wanting to leave the advertising business, she needed some time to rethink her career strategy and still have an income. A friend suggested that a flight attendant's flexible schedule might be the answer, so she applied and became a "sky goddess."

To become a successful flight attendant, Tracey relied upon her own strong character and social skills and underwent intense crisis management training, developing diverse communication skills to interact with many types of people. It was a position that stretched Tracey's abilities and comfort zone, starting her journey to becoming an expert communicator under pressure.

Imagine her surprise when she walked off an airplane one day to learn that her employer was going belly-up. Looking back, the signs were there, but at the time it came as a complete shock. Because she had moved out of state to take the job, unemployment benefits were unavailable and within weeks she was forced to apply for food stamps.

It was a humbling experience. The country was going through a recession and jobs were scarce. Tracey applied for any and every position, only to be told that her college education was a negative; she was over-qualified to work as a clerk or cashier. She and her roommate worked through temp agencies to make ends meet and cut every possible expense. To this day, she can still feed two people on one chicken for a week.

The gifts of this experience have been long-lasting. Tracey had to face the prospect of losing everything she held dear because she was financially and emotionally unprepared. Living in her comfortable bubble, refusing to acknowledge events and signs around her, cost her greatly. However, the upside was that she developed amazing levels of confidence and resilience. She lost her fear of being unemployed and the need for a guaranteed plan.

Today, when life starts to feel as though it is spinning out of control, Tracey remembers this period in her life as a stabilizing experience. She learned that enduring and thriving in the face of adversity was a choice, and that recognizing her options was empowering. Within three years of requiring public assistance,

Tracey recreated her career to become one of the first female executives at a five-star hotel company.

RECOGNIZING YOUR RESILIENCE

This exercise will help you recognize your resilience during past experiences.

1. Describe a past experience that was difficult. _____
   _____
   _____

2. What steps did you take to cope with it? _____
   _____
   _____

3. Which attitudes helped? _____
   _____
   _____

4. What other tools or skills did you use? _____
   _____
   _____

5. Where did you find strength? _____
   _____
   _____

6. Who helped you in the process?_____
   _____
   _____

7. How can you use these experiences to help yourself now?
   _____
   _____
   _____

MAKING ROOM FOR NEW OPPORTUNITIES

Making room for new opportunities in your life can be compared to cleaning out your refrigerator. You move things around, discard, rearrange and readjust so that you can put new things into it. The changes or losses in your life are making room for new opportunities; while it may be difficult to address the emptiness that was not there before, welcome the possibility of new and exciting events.

As you finish this chapter, take a deep breath and realize that through the introspective activities you have completed, you have more knowledge to deal with the not-known in a confident manner. With a deeper understanding of the way you made decisions in the past, you can make future decisions that are more compatible with a changing world. Understanding your expectations and attitudes plays an important role in your future planning and will help you adjust to the ongoing chaos of change.

Visualize letting go of past traditions, processes and the burden of old ways and entitlement. This will make room for new ways of living and thinking. Gather hopefulness and ideas; allow them to make way for your future life in the new norm. As you continue the process of building curiosity, flexibility and creativity skills, you will see the light at the end of the tunnel and, like Alice in Wonderland, you will emerge from the rabbit hole to make new discoveries about your career and personal life, the focus of our next chapter.

REMINDERS:

- Review past decisions for patterns, weaknesses and strengths.

- Understand how the not-known can influence your comfort zones.

- Identify hidden entitlement issues.

- Adapt a flexible attitude.

- Employ gratitude to shift your focus from negative to positive.

CHAPTER 3

CREATING THE MINDSET TO ADAPT AND PROSPER

Whatever you can do or dream you can, begin it.
Boldness has genius, power and magic in it.

~ Goethe

In the preceding chapter, you reviewed choices, decisions and attitudes that resulted in less-than-desirable outcomes in the past. As a result, some of your current situations may be difficult to tackle. In order to help you move beyond the chaos to identify the upside, this chapter guides you through the process of change. Contrary to traditional logic, preparing yourself for new circumstances begins with your inner self. Your first task will be to identify the habits, ideas and beliefs that have contributed to your present situation.

WORK ON THE INSIDE BEFORE THE OUTSIDE

Creating a mindset to adapt and prosper requires reinventing yourself from the inside out by learning to reframe the way you think and make decisions. Changing your thought process and personal beliefs can be challenging. Begin by being open to gaining more understanding, knowledge, support and the tools necessary to navigate through this demanding phase without fear. The upside is that you will make a transition and enjoy greater confidence in your actions and decisions.

The initial steps in the change process are becoming self-aware, cultivating the ability to listen closely to your inner voice, identifying recurring situations or patterns, and paying attention to your emotions during both positive and negative change. If you lose your job or savings, it is important to work through your negative emotions. You may feel ashamed, sad, guilty and frustrated. Refusing to face these emotions can lead to stress or depression, which negatively impacts your ability to think things through rationally and ultimately may affect your ability to respond appropriately in any new situation.

For example, the anger, desperation and negativity you are naturally experiencing might show through during your job interviews, which could set up a cycle of failure. A potential employer will recognize these negative signs and either pass you over for another candidate or hire you for a position with a limited future or potential, which only reinforces the negative cycle or downside.

To avoid or break this pattern, become more self-aware to determine the basis of your negative reaction and thoughts. Are you frustrated that no one seems willing to give you an opportunity to be successful? Does the situation support the negative belief that you'll never have the life you want or deserve? Are you afraid that you won't be able to re-establish the comfort of your former life? All of these are valid reactions to loss. Sort out the basis of your emotions, so that you can shift past them and create a more positive mindset.

> *There has been a shift from career consulting to an emphasis on transitions. I spend a lot of time building skills and self-esteem—helping them with closure, letting go of anger and to forgive.*
>
> ~ Judith Lansky, career consultant

The temptation may be strong to ignore this emotional identification step of the process; however, if you do, these feelings tend to recur. Until you take the time to address and specifically name them, they will undermine your ability to find comfort amid the not-known.

Sarah's Story

Sarah worked in healthcare for 10 years. Although she enjoyed a very good relationship with her supervisor, there was tension with one of the doctors she supported. Their communication and working relationship was strained, but they still managed to get the work done. And then, the unthinkable happened.

Sarah was completely shocked when she was let go from the job she loved by a supervisor she trusted. The initial blow put her into a dizzying state of confusion, anger and betrayal. She shut down her feelings, went into a panic about her finances and denial of her situation.

As a dual supporter in the family, Sarah's income was badly needed. Although friends and family came to her support, she refused to open up and discuss her feelings. She wasted several weeks in an emotional stew before finally acknowledging her anger and disappointment.

Part of the anger was directed at herself for not being smarter about communicating with the doctor who triggered her firing. Sarah had not considered the impact of a poor working relationship with an important player. It wasn't until she recognized the upside of this life lesson by addressing her own role in the termination that she was able to confront her fears and emotions. Once she forgave herself, she was able to move forward and find a new job.

Learn from Sarah's example. When you identify the root of a problem, only then are you able to create a positive solution. Take a moment to identify the feelings you are currently experiencing and write them down. Be honest with yourself and keep in mind that these emotions are temporary and a natural response. You do not have to like the way you feel, only acknowledge that these are honest reactions to your situation. Doing so usually helps take the edge off or decreases their intensity.

As you continue to practice self-awareness, notice how your inner perspectives and thoughts start to shift. Times of change are naturally times of growth if you look within. Sarah's growth involved letting go of her anger, examining her methods of dealing with conflict and finding a way to use her experience and skills. The upside of this process is that it eventually leads to enhancing your power core, or natural strengths and talents. When you develop clarity about your abilities, you begin to align choices and decisions with your authentic self and true life's work. Sarah was able to turn this negative situation around and uncover hidden talents that led to a new career. Her self-awareness and inner work helped her to become more authentic in dealing with conflicts and more empathetic toward others. These newly honed skills led her to a new job where she is using technology to help others decrease their stress.

Keep in mind that as the new norm continues to introduce change, your goal is to become more adaptive and comfortable. The upside is the ability to move out of existing chaos into a more sustainable career and personal life and to have a clearer sense of direction as you travel into the future. One of the greatest obstacles most people face on this journey is fear.

TIP #11

FEAR HAPPENS. FACE IT!

Because so much of the future is not-known, fear is a common and natural reaction. The current, unprecedented rate of change is causing many of you to experience unusual or significant upheavals in your life. To adapt and prosper, it is important to face your fears.

Recognizing that you have fears is a crucial first step. Self-awareness allows you to acknowledge and accept that you are feeling fear. The next step is to allow the feelings to surface and to notice what the fear is doing to you physically, as well as mentally. Are you stressed? Is your digestive system upset? Are you acting aggressively toward loved ones? Does it feel like the end of the life you have known? Are you worried that you won't ever recover from these feelings?

Your fear is an important call to action. Fear is rarely a solo reaction; it is a combination of feeling unsafe and threatened. As uncomfortable as these feelings are, they are warning you to stop, evaluate and shift gears.

DAVID'S STORY

For more than 10 years, David and his partners managed an apartment building for an owner who lived out of state. Because the property ran well and generated consistent revenue, David was stunned when the owner sold it to a developer who planned to sell the units as condominiums. Although he understood the business opportunity for the prior owner, emotionally, he felt punished for doing such a great job that it resulted in the elimination of his own position.

Over the next few weeks, David fell into depression. He felt a nagging sense of failure, even though the sale was not a reflection on his work ethic or abilities. It wasn't until his young son demanded some response that David finally broke down and admitted he was frightened. His wife recognized that David was grieving, and supported him by letting him take time to recover. Over the course of several months, David was finally able to open up and let all the sorrow and disappointment he was feeling come out. He now describes that process as pivotal in breaking through his fear of loss and freeing up his energy to pursue and enjoy new projects.

An upside to the process of releasing feelings is that you also release your mind from stress. Once you are free of stress, you are better able to uncover ideas, information and solutions which otherwise might be hidden. Keep in mind that acknowledging and addressing your fears actually enables you to work through and move beyond them. Fear, used correctly, can be a huge motivating factor. For David, facing his grief and the fear that he couldn't support his son motivated him out of his depression.

Unfortunately, there is no easy way to deal with fear. The only way out is to work through it; fear does not disappear without your participation. These feelings are not always comfortable, but as you allow them to surface and be released, they can motivate and guide you in your decision-making process. While you may not be able to eliminate your fear completely, you can choose to wallow in it or channel it in more positive directions. Using your fear as a positive motivator can actually decrease the intensity of those same fears. Once you've recognized it, fear can be a tool.

When you are in a state of fear, it's normal to want to avoid your feelings, distract yourself and go into denial. Unfortunately, burying or denying these feelings prevents you from moving forward. Just because you are in denial or avoidance of fear does not mean the feelings go away. If anything, they percolate beneath the surface, swallow your energy and keep you stuck. Avoidance only fuels fears and doubts. Remember, "What you resist, persists."

In spite of challenges and difficulties, individual and global change can also be a time of great opportunity to grow professionally, personally and spiritually. It is your choice. In order to understand your personal fear factors, including situations or people that cause you anxiety or fear, ask yourself:

- Am I afraid that I will never get out of the chaos?

- Am I concerned that I am letting others down?

- Is fear keeping me stuck in a familiar routine?

- Am I resistant to growing or embracing a new opportunity?

- Am I worried that my new success or happiness may create other problems?

- Am I focusing on what will happen if I fail, rather than what will happen if I succeed?

- Am I achieving my long-held objectives?

REALITY CHECK

There is a popular acronym for fear: False Evidence Appearing Real. This suggests that the concerns and thoughts you have are merely suggestions. While your fear may have a legitimate base in a past traumatic experience, the trauma has yet to repeat itself. Therefore, these fears haven't actually come to pass, which makes them "false." However, they certainly feel genuine, which gives them credibility and makes them "appear real."

It's natural to fear that something bad may happen, but what evidence do you have that it will or must happen? Are your fears credible? If so, have you researched the potential solutions to your fears or challenges? When presented with difficult situations in the past, have you been able to overcome them? Do you understand what skills are needed to move beyond your fears? Is this situation an opportunity to develop an inner strength for dealing with future changes that are bound to occur, or does the chaos feel more comfortable or normal than taking the steps to change?

PETER'S STORY

Peter's employer was relocating him once again. Even though he still enjoyed the work, years of constant relocation and change were beginning to take a toll on his personal life and sense of stability. As he began to accept that this was what his profession required, he also realized that he had a choice about how he would respond.

As he evaluated his skills, he recognized that he was good at building relationships with new clients and staff. He decided to use this natural ability to meet new friends, thereby improving his personal life. Peter also recognized that he needed more balance in his life to avoid burning out from the moves. He opted to slow down and to take care of himself by running, going to yoga classes and reading. Listening to his own fear and anxiety about the latest move proved to be a great reality check that allowed him to make positive changes in his life.

TIP #12

RESPOND VS. REACT

Change is inevitable in the not-known, and while you can't control the change that will develop in your life, you can control how you respond to it. To successfully adapt and prosper, it is helpful to remember that you always have a choice of behaviors with which to respond to anything that life presents. Initially, you may be tempted to react without considering the consequences; this is simply the result of old habits and behaviors getting in the way of your success and happiness. By remembering that you have choices you are able to make a thoughtful response instead.

Consider how you might respond differently to all the changes going on in your life if you were in complete control of them, or if they were your choice. For example, if you chose to change careers, as opposed to being fired or laid off, you would probably be less fearful, hopeless or angry. Although making a major life change can be uncomfortable and scary, it can also be energizing. Because the decision is yours, you may feel more in control of the situation.

Remember that you always have choices, regardless of the situation. No one is a victim of circumstance. There is no element of surprise to deal with when you choose to take action or make a decision, versus having change forced upon you. You may not like the options available to you, but there are choices nonetheless. Being conscious of this can give you a greater sense of empowerment and openness to new possibilities.

PEGGY'S STORY

Peggy chose to make changes and to take a leap of faith. Feeling stuck, stagnant and unfulfilled in her life, she wanted to start a life somewhere new and expand her work. Because she was self-employed, she could choose to work anywhere.

Her intuition and a few significant coincidences were pulling her toward Hawaii. Then, a close friend called out of the blue one day and asked Peggy to housesit her Hawaiian home for several months. Even though intellectually, the move seemed radical and a part of her felt it would be crazy, Peggy knew that staying in her current situation would only make her more miserable. As scary as it was, she was ready to take the leap. Despite her feelings of excitement and trepidation, she booked a one-way ticket to Hawaii and began to explore the islands.

Over the next year, her adventure led to new work, love, community and a home in Hawaii. In her journey of exploration,

Peggy found the courage to let go of the past and move out of her comfort zone into the not-known. An upside of creating a new life in Hawaii was that she also discovered more about herself. Peggy learned to trust her own intuition when making decisions. It opened her up to meeting new people and expanding her business. It was a risky move from the outside looking in, but well worth it from the inside out.

TIP #13

GO WITH THE FLOW

Have you ever met someone who, despite the external situations around them, always seems to bounce back on their feet? These people understand how to make unexpected change work for them, instead of resisting it. Flexibility and resilience are two of the tools you can use to flow with change, instead of fighting an uphill battle. Flowing means experiencing the present moment, instead of worrying about the future. To do this requires trust and a lot of practice. A helpful mantra is *the power of pause*. At any given moment, stop what you are doing—pause—and get in touch with what is happening around you and what you are feeling from within.

> *When we go with the flow, we put ourselves in a position of acceptance and learning. It is not about intellectualizing. It is about allowing experiences to guide you where you need to go.*
>
> ~ Dr. Kimberly Ventus-Darks

When Jody tried this exercise after losing her job, she realized that the feelings of fear and loss were similar to another time of loss in her life—her divorce. She acknowledged her feelings and used self-awareness to stay in the present moment, focus on her current surroundings and not reminisce about her past life. This practice of observing your own feelings and behaviors allows you to better respond to any situation.

Trust that you will make the right choices and that with change comes opportunity. Establishing this trust may feel counterintuitive, but keep affirming to yourself that you are moving in the right direction. Practicing this type of mental flexibility will allow you to believe that you will find the answers and a clear direction. The upside of surrender and flow is that you begin to see opportunities and choices. By releasing your attachment to what you think the outcome should be, you allow more opportunities and creative solutions to present themselves.

The opposite of flow is when you feel you need to be in control of outcomes. When you try to control the events and lives around you, you are actually limiting yourself. If you choose to be more open and trust the life process, there are often endless opportunities and solutions available to you that are hidden when you take a rigid stance. For instance, you may be attached to getting one specific job or position at work, because it is within your comfort zone. When you release the need to control the process, you may find a better job you would not have considered before. Try letting go of the need to control. When you do, you open the door to opportunities that may serve your needs better and expand your skill set.

Flowing and flexibility mean letting go of preconceived ideas, expectations and the "shoulds" in your life. For example, if you hold on to a career or lifestyle that no longer is possible or sustainable, it limits your opportunities for the future. The ability to adapt to new and changing life conditions gives you the strength and wisdom to find answers to your questions and the next steps in your life. It expands your horizons by opening you up to a larger perspective and outlook.

Rate Your Flexibility Quotient (FQ)

Rate each of your responses to the statements below on a scale from 1 to 5 with **1** being "not at all like me" and **5** being "very much like me."

_____ 1. I prefer to be in control of situations and people around me.

_____ 2. I find it difficult to adapt to change.

_____ 3. I'd like my life to remain the same.

_____ 4. I feel physical stress when presented with a new opportunity or change.

_____ 5. I resist people and situations that threaten my reality and comfort zone.

_____ 6. I find last minute changes stressful.

_____ 7. When in a group, I tend to wait for people to ask my opinion.

_____ 8. I enjoy having a routine schedule.

_____ 9. Stability is very important to me.

_____ 10. It matters to me that people respect the quality of my work.

_____ 11. I worry about what to say to people I don't know well.

_____ 12. I am concerned that people critique or judge me.

_____ 13. Surprises can interrupt my routine or plan.

Now tally the total sum of your responses and determine your FQ as follows:

13-26 You are doing a terrific job of facing your fears and being flexible.

27-45 You are holding your own, but feel stressed by new changes. Keep working.

46-65 You are headed for a meltdown.

VERONICA'S STORY

One day, Veronica arrived home after a long day at work to discover that her beautiful townhouse and everything inside had been destroyed by fire. Without warning, everything she valued was lost.

After a mind-numbing week of shock, grief and dealing with insurance companies, Veronica was able to step back and take an honest inventory of her life, despite the overwhelming situation. As she looked back, she was surprised to realize that she had felt trapped in her life and home situation, and had actually wanted to move for some time, but old memories had made it difficult to let go. Rather than being courageous and taking the necessary action on her own terms, the fire forced her to make the move.

Had she been more honest with herself, Veronica would have begun researching new places to live long before the fire, and the transition would have been must easier. Looking back, she can see that the fire, although traumatic at the time, was a liberating experience. It forced her to make the changes she so deeply wanted and allowed her to create a new life for herself. She also recognized that attachment to possessions was part of her old identity. She now has a new relationship with her material belongings; although they are important, they do not identify her.

Another important upside is that Veronica has learned to both listen to and honor her inner thoughts and conversations, and to use them to be proactive in making changes. She chose to use this life experience as one of growth, a way to focus on the positive and to view it as a gift. These lessons were vital to move to the next phase of her life.

TRANSFORM CHANGE INTO PERSONAL UPSIDES

Another way to view and experience transition is by making a conscious effort to uncover the positive aspects that have occurred as a result of the changes in your life. Think about a life change that was forced upon you, over which you had no control. Chances are that you remember the painful and sad outcomes of this experience first. Now give yourself a moment to reflect on possible upsides. Consider the following examples:

- You lost a demanding job where you put in long hours. The upside is that you now have more time for yourself, family and other activities. Knowing this and recognizing that you still need a job, you can look for work that fulfills your needs, yet allows for more free time than your previous job. You may even choose to find work that encourages fulfillment of family or community relationships.

- A spouse or partner has ended your relationship. The upside may be a realization that you were spending much of your focus and energy maintaining a relationship that wasn't working. Feel the grief of the loss and examine where you may need to grow and perhaps take better care of yourself. Maybe the time and freedom you now have will support you in moving into a new home, job or hobby that the relationship did not allow.

- You were forced to file bankruptcy after losing your life savings. A possible upside may be the chance to evaluate your approach to money and consumption, to identify your values and priorities and to develop a better financial plan.

- You lost a job in which you were secure and had a good skill set. The upside is that the situation forced you to explore other aspects of your field. This can lead to new training and a skill set that commands a higher salary or greater satisfaction in your work.

- You were required to relocate to a small town from a city. The upside is the sense of community that small towns offer.

- Your hours were cut back. The upside is the chance to improve your health and relationships by not working long hours.

The point is that your perspective can change even with setbacks, if you look for the upside.

THE DOWNSIDE OF EXPECTATIONS

To fully flow with change, it is also important to examine how your expectations and attachments to outcomes or results can act as potential barriers to your success. Holding on to preconceived ideas and expectations can limit your ability to take advantage of existing possibilities. You may miss opportunities because your expectations lead you in a different direction. For example, if you expect to get the same salary increase each year, you may overlook other ways to excel in your career. You may be able to build your income by stepping back, assessing other opportunities and putting your energy there. When you expect something to happen and it doesn't, it's normal to feel a tremendous letdown. If your expectations are unrealistic or unsubstantiated, they can set you up for potential failure.

In the new economy and world of global change, there is no certainty. You may discover that there is more of a need to research your decisions in ways you were not anticipating. Some of your prior experience may apply to your new situations or you may need to reinvent them, depending on what the new expectations of you are. Remember, the not-known is the new norm. Letting go of your expectations and attachments to outcomes is an important step in your quest for clarity.

HOW DO EXPECTATIONS AFFECT MY LIFE?
ANSWER THE FOLLOWING QUESTIONS.

1. What expectations did I have before my current crisis?

    _____

    _____

    _____

2. What past expectations have led me to disappointments?

    _____

    _____

    _____

3. What are my current expectations? _____

    _____

    _____

4. What ideas am I committed to and unwilling to change?

    _____

    _____

    _____

IDENTIFYING YOUR POSITION IN THE TRANSITION PROCESS

Executive coach and author Patricia Varley is an expert at working with individuals in transition. Varley recommends understanding the following stages of transition in order to navigate through your own personal and professional experiences. These descriptions are loosely based on William Bridges' pioneering book, *Transitions: Making Sense of Life's Changes*. According to Bridges, most people experience: 1) Endings, 2) the Neutral Zone, and 3) New Beginnings.

Endings or letting go of the past can cause feelings of loss, grief or nostalgia. Whether you are experiencing a divorce, loss of a job or a move across the country, letting go of what is and what was evokes a variety of feelings. As painful and frightening as this process may be, it is a necessary step in moving forward. You must let go of the old in order to fully experience the new. Resist the urge to rush through endings; allow yourself time to complete this work before beginning the next phase.

The **Neutral Zone** or period of uncertainty can feel scary, like being in the fog of the unknown. It can feel chaotic or it can feel as though you are in limbo, simply treading water. However, it is an important time of reflection to determine who you are and what you want. It prepares you for the next stage.

For example, if you are newly single after many years of marriage, you may feel uncomfortable, unclear and isolated. You may wonder whether there is a way out or even a new life or relationship ahead. Be patient and have faith that you can create a life that is meaningful. The Neutral Zone is your incubation time as you prepare for new beginnings.

New beginnings are the time to start a new career, a creative endeavor or a personal relationship; to volunteer; to live a healthier life; or to retire. It can be an exciting period as you reinvent yourself and redesign your life. These powerful times of change, renewal and discovery can lead to a deeper sense of self and transformation. You feel energized, excited and eager to move forward. New beginnings occur throughout your lifetime.

After reviewing the stages of transition, ask yourself:

1. Where do I find myself in the stages of transition? ____

   _____

   _____

2. How do I feel about change and transition?_____

   _____

   _____

3. Am I resistant to it?_____

4. Can I embrace it, perceive things differently and shift my behavior to adjust to the changes in my industry or in my personal and family relations? _____

Remember to be kind to yourself during these stages of transition. Experiencing increased mental exertion can take a toll on you physically. Extra sleep, a balanced diet and exercise will help you maintain an objective perspective.

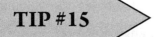
TIP #15

LIGHTEN THE LOAD WITH HUMOR

During times of great difficulty, finding the lightness of being and humor in your situation goes a long way toward easing transition. Scientists have determined that laughing is primal and one of our first means of communication. Babies laugh long before they speak. No one has to teach them how to laugh.

Can you find anything funny about your situation? Sometimes, when life feels so out of control, all we can do is laugh. The upside is that the laughter releases endorphins to alleviate your stress level. When you can physically release some of the tension and focus away from your problems, the challenges become less frightening. Take your mind off pressing concerns by watching a funny sitcom, spending an afternoon with a friend, or playing some games.

Stephen lost his job, and his son was in trouble at school. With so many calamities on his plate, he thought that things couldn't get any worse. They did. His car broke down and two days later, the roof developed a sizeable leak. With no options in sight, Stephen started to laugh. While laughing didn't solve anything, it was a relief from all the upheaval and an opportunity to feel free from some of the extreme pressure.

Look for the humor in your situation. Laugh a little. Laughter can be a powerful tool during transition.

MAKING THE MOVE FORWARD

Sometimes, change seems to happen overnight. Even events that we should have seen coming—like the bankruptcy of an employer—can come as a complete shock. It takes a while for human beings to adapt to abrupt change. Research shows that changing habits and thought patterns takes 21 to 28 days for your brain to adjust. You can't revamp your thought process overnight. Incorporating these ideas and suggestions will take time to feel comfortable and natural. Nurture yourself on a daily basis during this process by consciously thinking, journaling and spending time looking for gradual changes. After a few weeks, you should start to see and feel differently about your progress.

Mandy shared a success story in shifting her thought process that was so gradual she almost missed it. An interior design consultant, she gave clients access to her personal phone numbers. Mandy was eating breakfast early one morning when the phone rang; it was one of her more important clients, who required a lot of attention and reassurance. Mandy glanced at her watch as she answered the phone, and then calmly informed her client she would call back in 30 minutes.

The shift was so subtle that Mandy did not even become conscious of the change in her behavior until she finished her breakfast. It was then that she realized the "old" Mandy would have dropped everything on the spot to reassure her client and put her own needs on the back burner. As it turned out, Mandy's client was perfectly fine by the time Mandy called back; it wasn't a situation that Mandy needed to handle after all.

When you allow yourself time to integrate new desires and directions, the changes can be subtle and more natural. What's important to recognize is that you are indeed making progress, however understated it may appear.

Whether you like it or not, change happens in spite of you. The more you can accept and embrace these times and opportunities, the easier it will be and the more success you'll have. This is a time to grow and evolve to a level you have never experienced before.

Hopefulness is a step toward radical faith and trust, which is key in navigating through times of change and uncertainty.

Use this as a time to hone your skills, address your barriers, dream, imagine, and work toward a new life. Marcel Proust wrote, "Life isn't about traveling to different landscapes, but seeing with different eyes." How you choose to see the transitions in your life using the tools in this chapter will help you achieve empowered and conscious change. Next begins the journey of redefining the landscape through different eyes by exploring how to achieve your success in a changing world.

REMINDERS

- **Confront your fears.**

- **Flow with the change.**

- **Be flexible in your approach.**

- **Use your resilience.**

- **Be positive and grateful.**

- **Lose your expectations and attachments.**

- **Keep a sense of humor.**

- **Allow yourself time to experience and explore these stages.**

CHAPTER 4

ACHIEVING SUSTAINABLE SUCCESS AND HAPPINESS IN A CHANGING WORLD

Happiness is not a destination. It is the attitude with which you choose to travel.

~ Yogi Arit Desal

Mankind has explored the topics of success and happiness throughout our existence. These elusive concepts are unique for each individual. It is entirely possible to be happy without success and to be successful without happiness. In this chapter, we explore how the decline of the American Dream redefines your success expectations and goals. Ultimately, this process affects your happiness.

REWORK YOUR AMERICAN DREAM

Although facing the loss of a job or lifestyle may seem difficult enough, in order to thrive in the new reality, it is important also to deal with the loss of your success model and to change it to something new. Give yourself the chance to mourn the loss and then acknowledge that you have the power to find happiness and success.

We have discussed how the new norm is impacting our traditional thinking of the American way of life. What was materially achievable and available for the previous generation is now difficult to accomplish. It will be even more difficult for subsequent generations. While the concept of prosperity and living a full life is still a part of our culture, a shift is required to clarify your own personal expectations and dreams. If you believe that the old paradigm of the American Dream isn't sustainable, the next step for you is to revaluate your model.

This New American Dream assignment is designed to acquaint you with a sustainable success model—another way of working and living that might bring happiness and success and will probably not be consumer-driven.

In the past, success was tied to how much money, power or status a person had. Consciously or unconsciously, at some time in your life, you developed ideal models for success and happiness that are impacting your career and lifestyle choices today. Consider the people and relationships that helped you define these models. When you look at past influencers like your parents or other adult role models, how are they holding up today?

REALITY EXERCISE PART 1

1. What were your parents' values and how have they influenced your choices for a successful life? _____

    _____

    _____

2. Describe their model for success. Which aspects of that model did you adopt? _____

    _____

    _____

3. Describe the lifestyle in which you were raised. _____

    _____

    _____

4. Who else influenced your definition of success or happiness? _____

    _____

5. What influences have brought you to the success model you currently hold or to which you are aspiring? _____

    _____

6. How would you rate your level of happiness and success?

    _____

    _____

Social influences also impact your definition of success and happiness. Messages come to you by way of friends and peers, as well as print and Internet ads, television commercials, billboards, TV shows, movies and even social networking sites. Most of these messages portray people enjoying a wealthy lifestyle and imply that the advertised product will make you successful and happy.

It has been popular to boast about purchases of perceived status symbols as achievements worthy of celebration. This has created a subliminal, unconscious message that success is directly related to the acquisition of goods. It also reinforces your human tendency to compare yourself to others, a practice that can negatively impact your self-esteem and happiness. A much healthier and more satisfying practice is to focus on your own personal achievements.

REALITY EXERCISE PART 2

1. Have you ever compared your life to that of a friend or family member? Was your appraisal positive or negative? Does this impact your relationship with this person? _____

    _____

    _____

2. Are your family and/or friends supportive of your success? Do you share your less-than-successful ventures with the people closest to you? Why or why not? _____

    _____

    _____

3. Do you think you are happier, less happy or about as happy as the people in your social circle and work setting? _____

    _____

4. What would you do with your life if money were no concern? _____

    _____

Although an economic downturn may have changed the way you spend money, has it affected your perception of success? Have you heard people talk about cutting back on current spending and job expectations, while in their minds, they may be waiting for the downturn to end, so they can return to their old lifestyle? Even if the economy does not bounce back, there is an upside: you can still be successful and happy by adjusting your perceptions.

If your vision of success can no longer be achieved in the new norm, how will you cope with it and turn it around? Use the following exercise to begin to redefine success and happiness.

DEFINITION QUESTIONNAIRE:

1. I felt successful when _____

    _____

2. If the economy, job opportunities and salaries stay at the present level, what factors/realities will influence my definition of success? _____

    _____

3. What factors that I consider part of my success and happiness definition are missing in my life now? _____

    _____

    _____

4. I get really excited about my life when _____

    _____

    _____

5. I am happiest when _____

_____

6. If I knew I could not fail, I would _____

_____

_____

TIP #17

RELEASE WHEN/THEN THINKING

How many times have you told yourself that when you reach a certain weight, financial level, or some other goal, *then* you'll feel happy? This "when/then" thinking can trap you in a holding pattern of discontent, where success and happiness are never within reach, always one "when" away. Understanding how success and happiness are intertwined can release you from this negative pattern and accelerate your goals. Sonja Lyubomirsky explains, "It's not that happiness comes from success. It's that happiness also creates success; it's a causal circle."

A substantial amount of research has been conducted on the subject of happiness, and the findings may surprise you. Once basic needs are met, research indicates that people don't become happier with increased income. What seems to matter more than money is having good friends and family and the time to spend on social activities. Studies by Sonja Lyubomirsky, Kennon Sheldon and David Schaade suggest that 50 percent of our happiness comes from genetic factors; 40 percent from our habitual thoughts, feelings, words and actions; and, only ten percent from circumstances such as wealth, martial status and a good job. The point is that money does not buy happiness.

In order to break the when/then pattern, begin celebrating small, insignificant moments of your day like finding a great parking spot, hearing from a friend, getting a task finished on time. The key is to diminish the lofty "when" by transitioning to the present moment of "now." As you celebrate small achievements, notice your reaction. Does it alleviate some of your stress? Is your outlook more optimistic? Do you feel empowered?

Your personal success and happiness model

Redefining and updating your personal success and happiness models can also weaken the when/then habit. Use the following questions and activities to help you get started in the process of redefining your success and happiness models:

1. How can you integrate the new reality with holistic definitions of success and happiness? _____

    _____

    _____

2. How can you shape your career and lifestyle choices in order to create greater success and happiness. Try not to rely upon previous models or the models of others?_____

    _____

    _____

3. Do your core values fit with the new norm? Explain. _____

    _____

    _____

    _____

4. Can you identify individuals whose models for success and happiness are more closely associated with today's realities?

_____

_____

5. What characteristics do these individuals possess?_____

_____

_____

6. Can you identify with any of them when defining a new model for yourself? _____

_____

NOTES ON WHAT THIS EXERCISE REVEALED FOR ME:

_____

_____

_____

JUDY'S STORY

While Judy was working in a corporate environment, she negotiated a flexible working schedule to meet the demands of a single parent. Then, her supervisor changed and he eliminated her flexible schedule, insisting that face time was important. Because Judy believed she had no options, she stayed in the position even though she was very unhappy. Her success model was fostered by her parent's values—*you stay committed to your job, no matter what*!

Missing time with her kids was causing Judy a great deal of stress, and she was often moody and unproductive. Realizing that they did not fit with her new reality, she began to question her parent's values. Still, the worry over leaving a good-paying job was a constant conflict.

Eventually, the pain of staying became too great and Judy began to see that she did indeed have options. She relied upon supportive friends and professional acquaintances to explore her other alternatives. As she considered the pros and cons and calculated that she had enough savings to last a year, Judy took a risk and left her job to start an entrepreneurial enterprise.

A HAPPINESS JOURNAL

To help you understand what factors influence how happy you are, start a happiness journal. Begin by recognizing small instances of joy or satisfaction, and then reflect upon the times in your life when you were the happiest. What were the reasons for your happiness? Did you feel a sense of freedom? Were you surrounded by people who completely loved and accepted you? In contrast, think of the events or experiences that caused you to be unhappy. Why did you remain or participate in those situations? Ask yourself, what was the belief that caused you personal pain and suffering?

> *The real enemy of happiness is the mind's fixations and delusions. Look at the situation differently; see the truth, and the suffering is less. If you have the right mind, you can overcome anything—you can be happy, no matter what.*
> ~ The State Oracle of Tibet

GINA'S STORY

There were many losses in Gina's life. Because of divorce, she lost an entire lifestyle: husband, stepson and home. During the difficult transition, she realized that she had given up friendships because of her husband's jealousy. Her supportive friends were important to her, so she decided to move across the country to be near them.

Gina possessed great resilience and flexibility; she chose to see her move not as a hardship, but as an exciting challenge. Her frugal nature was a great help. To prepare for the transition, she sold or gave away many personal items, withdrew her savings, packed her car and headed across country. As a freelance artist and host of children's parties, Gina's chosen career allowed her to move anywhere she chose.

The first year was often lonely, but it gave her an opportunity to clarify her happiness and success models. She reconnected with old friends, reflected upon her losses and started from the ground up. By thinking and journaling, Gina concluded that she felt most successful and happiest when she was helping others, especially children.

She decided to go back to school to obtain the required certification that would allow her to be a substitute teacher and work in after-school programs. With her new-found freedom, she had time to supplement her income by starting a new business creating and selling unique soaps and candies. By clarifying all of her values, Gina also found a new life partner who shared her beliefs.

EXTRINSIC VS. INTRINSIC MODELS

Most people find they are happiest when both intrinsic and extrinsic values mesh. An intrinsic value is a belief that is essential to your nature, such as showing gratitude or appreciation, or following the Golden Rule of treating others as you would want to be treated. Intrinsic values tend to be internally motivated and may provide a deeper meaning in the long term. Extrinsic values originate externally; for example, creating a beautiful environment in which to live and work. Extrinsic factors tend to be short-lived or temporary.

There are times when your intrinsic values are influenced extrinsically and vice-versa. The long-term sustainability of your happiness depends on understanding which ones are truly intrinsic. While extrinsic factors may bring you joy or gratification at the time, in general, they do not promote long-lasting happiness.

At a recent workshop based on this book, a hairdresser related a story about one of her clients that illustrates what happens when intrinsic and extrinsic beliefs are confused. The hairdresser had worked with a male client for more than a decade. Over the years, the man's hair began to thin, to the point of creating a bald spot. One day, the client reprimanded the hairdresser for giving him bad haircuts that "made him look bald." The hairdresser was stunned. The gentleman never once considered that he was losing his hair, but blamed an external factor, the hairdresser. Apparently, the client had both a bald spot and a self-assessment blind spot.

What internal factors do you require to be happy or feel successful? When these factors are missing, do you ever find yourself reaching for something extrinsic? For example, do you ever find yourself shopping or spending time at the mall when you are upset, depressed or confused? What extrinsic "bald spots" do you suspect exist in your definitions of success and happiness?

SUCCESS BELIEF SYSTEM QUESTIONNAIRE

Use these questions to evaluate the way you view success.

1. Do you have meaningful relationships with your family members? Friends? Spouse or partner? Co-workers? _____

2. Do you contribute to your community?_____

3. Are you able to enjoy the moment?_____

4. Do you have moments of gratitude? _____

5. Do you make the time to be compassionate when dealing with friends, family, co-workers and others? _____

6. Do you participate in ongoing learning for self-improvement? _____

7. Do you exercise regularly? _____

8. Do you volunteer or help others in your community?_____

9. Do you have a spiritual practice? _____

10. Do you vote and/or participate in local or national government activities? _____

11. Do you avoid comparisons with others? _____

12. Are you socially, environmentally and politically conscious?

_____

13. Do you have meaningful work, or are you looking for work to provide for your basic needs, such as food, shelter, clothing and healthcare?_____

The new American Dream will be different, and so will your success model. That doesn't mean it won't be meaningful. In fact, it may be more comfortable and less stressful than trying to live up to obsolete models. The question is, what realistic model will make you feel successful and happy? What can you live with? What attitudes need to change? What is sustainable?

> *Try not to become a man of success, but rather try to become a man of value.*
>
> ~ Albert Einstein

HAPPINESS BELIEF MODEL EXERCISE

Based on concepts presented in this chapter, answering the questions below will help you lay the foundation for a new belief model.

1. Which of your core values are important to act on daily, such as keeping balance, being aware or something else?

   _____

   _____

2. I will be happy when _____

   _____

   _____

3. What daydreams of happiness keep floating through your mind and don't seem to go away? _____

   _____

4. What gives you energy when you do it? _____

   _____

   _____

5. What is it about this activity that motivates you to feel this way? _____

   _____

6. If you had your life to live over, what would you say or do differently? _____

_____

_____

7. Why? _____

_____

Read through your answers to the success and happiness belief model exercises to develop your own scenarios. These are just a few examples:

- Making enough money to live comfortably, but not extravagantly

- Meeting challenges (loss of money, family crisis, health issues) with optimism and good problem solving

- Having time to develop meaningful friendships

- Nurturing a spiritual life with reflection and prayer

- Finding inexpensive ways to experience other cultures

- Disciplining impulses for overspending, overeating or other indulgences and addictions

- Appreciating nature and simple things

- Spending time in a creative mode crafting, creating artwork, or writing

- Participating in local and national government activities

- Giving back to the community by empowering others

- Maintaining a healthy body and lifestyle

NOW WRITE YOUR DEFINITION OF SUCCESS

Based on the exercises and examples from this chapter, define what success means for you in the new norm: _____

_____

_____

_____

_____

_____

_____

Abe Lincoln said, "Most people are about as happy as they make their minds up to be." Part of the happiness and success process is making a conscious choice to be happy regardless of your circumstances. Happiness doesn't happen overnight; it is a work in progress, with highs and lows.

These exercises will take you on a journey of self-discovery, with both surprises and disappointments. Your discoveries, no matter how small or large, are important ingredients for creating sustained success. You'll have the opportunity in following chapters to continue this process and start implementing your new belief system into a plan of action. In the meantime, revisit this chapter frequently to develop and reinforce your new ideals.

> *When we are no longer able to change a situation, we are challenged to change ourselves.*
> ~ Victor Frankl

REMINDERS

- **Reevaluate the American Dream and your definition of success.**

- **Be aware of values and influences in your definition.**

- **Understand the relationship between success and happiness.**

- **Look for new role models.**

- **Redefine success based on the new norm.**

- **Make happiness a conscious decision.**

CHAPTER 5

TRANSFORMING YOUR PASSION INTO A SUSTAINABLE CAREER

Viewing freedom as intrinsic to our being, we discover that our lives are what we make of them. All options are open, our choices unlimited. When we have knowledge, space grants us unbounded opportunity and time presents us with infinite possibilities for change.

~ Tarthang Tulku

"I love what I do!" How many people can make that simple statement? If you can't, what will it take for you to be truly passionate about your chosen career or work? When you are able to determine a career path that brings you joy, can you be assured that it will be sustainable over the long term? Will the industry or your business last six months, one year, five years or more? How does a rapidly changing economy affect what you do? What trends, patterns, and data are you basing your career decisions upon? If you had to predict how long your career or work will last, what would you say? Transforming your passion into a sustainable career requires that you address these questions.

TIP #18

MAKE YOUR PASSION YOUR TRUE POWER

No one is born knowing what they want to do or achieve in life. Some of us decide at a very early age and follow through on that youthful dream. For the rest of us, vision and clarity take longer. We glimpse joy and enthusiasm but are not blessed with a clear path.

There's a lot of information available on finding and identifying your passion, but what does passion really mean? For the purpose of creating a sustainable life and career, we define passion as a strong feeling for an area of interest that absorbs your focus, brings you joy and fills you with a sense of purpose. It's important to note, too, that your passions evolve and change throughout your life.

We realize that passion is not the only component necessary for developing a successful career, yet it provides the energy to meet your monetary needs and daily living responsibilities. By identifying your passions now, you avoid pursuing unsustainable paths that can lead to a never-ending cycle of disappointment and dissatisfaction.

The chaos of change can provide the opportunity to start reconnecting with activities, skills and tasks that bring pleasure—the ones in which hours go by before you know it. In Chapter 2, you encountered techniques that took you out of you comfort zone and triggered your imagination and creativity.

In this chapter, you will engage your mind, body and spirit to find work that makes you want to get up earlier in the morning. Think about the knowledge you have attained by venturing out of your comfort zone. Remember that breakdowns always create an upside—a possibility for breakthroughs.

> *Accept slow time as a gift.*
> ~ Robin Sheerer, career expert

If you aren't working now and are looking for a job, you have a great opportunity to engage in activities that promote creativity. Use the time to uncover ideas that lead you in a new direction and are meaningful. This doesn't mean you stop looking for ways to cover your expenses, but it does mean giving yourself permission to investigate options and not settle on something that gives you no joy.

If you are working or in transition and aren't happy with your career or work, set aside time for activities that can lead you to more purpose and joy. One option is to organize your own Dream Team, a supportive sounding board to explore new opportunities. Criteria and guidelines for beginning a Dream Team are found in Chapter 9.

GETTING STARTED

To find your passion, you must let go, release all expectations and surrender yourself to your innermost feelings. In Chapter 2, you made a list of core values, the things that are important to you. Using this list as a springboard, you can now start identifying what makes you passionate. This is an important discipline in the process of moving forward and creating sustainable work.

If your personal core values are missing, eventually, the work becomes incongruent and you either burn out or have to begin searching for new opportunities all over again.

It is also essential to encourage your thought process without criticism. Don't judge your thoughts; acknowledge whatever ideas come forward. Be open to the mysterious and the unexpected.

Think about favorite activities you enjoyed as a child. What qualities made these events so cherished? Are these qualities present in any of your hobbies, tasks, or activities now? What elements of your current escape activities make you passionate? For example, if you play golf, what is it that you enjoy or love about golf? Is it the mental competition with yourself and others? Is it the physical satisfaction of driving the ball? Or, is it the camaraderie of being in a foursome? Focus on the qualities of each memory and activity that make you excited and eager to participate.

Most importantly, write your thoughts down in a journal. Don't depend on your memory. Discuss these thoughts with someone you trust to be objective and who can help you decipher commonalities and traits. Ask for feedback and observations from friends and family. Sometimes, the obvious is clear to everyone but you. Patterns will emerge. Uncovering your passion takes time; it is a process. Keep your journal close by.

QUESTIONS TO CONSIDER IN IDENTIFYING YOUR PASSIONS:

1. What aspects of past jobs have given you joy? _____

   _____

2. What tasks or activities have you enjoyed where you lost track of time? _____

   _____

3. What aspects of past jobs have drained you of energy or created stress? _____

4. How long have you typically stayed at a job? _____

5. What has caused you to seek other employment, when voluntary? _____

   _____

6. What mutual core values have you sought from an employer? _____

7. Upon arriving at work, have you been focused on tasks or begun the day by socializing? _____

8. Have external factors been important to you: for example, working near natural light or a quiet atmosphere that allows concentration? _____

9. How important has external feedback been to your work?

   _____

10. What impact have deadlines played in your productivity?

    _____

11. What time of day has found you most energetic: morning, afternoon or evening? _____

12. If money were no object, what career would you choose?

    _____

Answering these questions can lead you to uncover your most fulfilling career path.

Even though uncovering passion is an important part of finding a sustainable career, don't give up looking for work that falls into the category of stimulating and meaningful. Alternatively, you may have to find work that will temporarily put bread on the table. Remember, too, that passion can be found in your personal life.

CAROLYN'S STORY: USING THE PAST TO IDENTIFY PASSIONS

After marrying and gaining an instant family with two small children, Carolyn's public relations career needed a change. Working weekends and late nights did not jibe with her new role of wife and mother. But PR was all Carolyn knew; she had no idea what she could do instead.

She set out to find a new career with intense, deliberate thought, asking herself lots of questions. What job would hold her interest? What skills did she bring to the table? What aspects of her job did she *not* like? What type of job was realistic in her town, which was largely a retirement community? She studied her resume, placing previous jobs in one of two columns: positive vs. negative.

For two months, Carolyn allowed her mind to wander over past positions—the exhilarating ones and those that were draining. She attempted to identify the specific tasks or events that made her feel strongly one way or another, and placed them in the appropriate column. Allowing time for her ideas to germinate was crucial to the process. While the more dramatic events would be fresher in her mind, she needed to allow herself some time to recall the more subtle factors.

One thing was certain, any work that required significant amounts of solitude was not a good fit; she liked to be surrounded by people. The more subtle factors surprised her. She identified two skills that were common in her past jobs, which she loved—the ability to communicate under pressure and speaking to groups. Carolyn researched career opportunities that would allow her to use these skills, and the result was a 15-year career as a trainer, motivational speaker and executive presentations skills coach.

The biggest strength of this exercise is that it reveals common skills and activities you usually take for granted. Because these abilities are easy for you, you don't value them or appreciate that others don't possess them. You overlook their value, but then miss them when you no longer have the opportunities to exercise them. Pinpointing your likes and dislikes will reveal your natural strengths and abilities and highlight hidden motivators and passions waiting to be ignited.

JOB JOURNAL TIPS

- Designate a specific time to write in your job journal. Reflect for a few minutes at this same time every day until you train your mind to automatically focus on the exercise.

- Before you go to sleep at night, ask your subconscious to send you ideas on what makes the ideal job for you. Keep a pen and paper by the bed and write down any thoughts that occur throughout the night or first thing in the morning.

- When work memories, past conversations or images appear, ask yourself what purpose that experience served and write it in your journal.

- This process takes a minimum of three to four weeks to work through. Relax and enjoy the process.

- Study your responses at the end of a few weeks to see what commonalities, environments and qualities are needed to create the ideal work for you.

Your passions may change over time; what was important earlier in your life may not be so now. Be open to that change and don't hold on to work or a profession that has no value to you now.

DEBORAH'S STORY: INSTILLING PASSION IN A PROFESSION

From the time she was eight years old, Deborah's passion was to dance, and for 10 years it was her profession. Due to family circumstances and her spouse's illness, her career as a professional dancer ended before she was ready to bow out. It was time to let go and direct her creativity and passion in a career better suited to her new situation and economic reality, as she was now the breadwinner of the family.

Today, her passion for dance is still strong, but not as a profession—it's now a hobby. Deborah integrated creative movement classes into a new career as a Montessori teacher, which allowed her to share her joy with children. Exploring new realms, techniques and styles of dance brings excitement and joy to her personal life. Her interest in flamenco dance took her to Spain and new cultures, and that experience brought new energy to her career and personal life.

In the new norm, chances are high that you will have many passions and careers. Building on past career experiences and identifying your passion for them is a way to move forward to a new opportunity or path. The next story illustrates a transition from corporate employee to small business owner.

KAREN'S STORY: TRANSITIONING SKILLS AND UNCOVERING A PASSION

Karen recalls that it could have been labeled a midlife crisis, but she was fed up with working in corporate America and wanted to do something more purposeful. She took a risk and left her corporate training job. With enough money put aside and her husband's job, she could afford some time to discover a career that would use her skills and be more satisfying.

As she reflected upon her career, Karen remembered her struggle and frustration at trying to juggle her personal and professional lives. As a stepmother, she felt great empathy for working-women with children and their need for support services in the workplace. Many of her core values had to do with balance, flexibility and time for family, so she wanted to find a new career that would incorporate these interests and values.

To supplement her income, Karen did some part-time research for a filmmaker looking for industrial topics. He suggested she study demographics and economic articles to identify emerging workplace patterns in the U.S. Many of the materials she read talked about women entering the workplace.

Karen became passionate about the need to help mothers in this situation. It was the beginning of an idea she shared with many friends and professional colleagues. She joined a mentoring support group that met regularly to develop new business ideas, and they encouraged her. The more she talked about it, the more positive feedback she got. Karen continued to research, read, daydream and visualize the project. To keep her creative juices going, she took on some creative writing as an outlet.

Karen began to develop a business model for helping working women that included consulting and other products and services. Networking, she met a woman who was investigating a similar idea. That meeting ignited a new business that provided strategic planning and training aimed at corporate human resources. It has lasted several decades, given her great joy, and allowed her to create and change directions when the needs of the workplace changed.

When developing your ideas, be sure to incorporate flexibility into your business or career plan. If the need for your services, products or skills should change, how can you adapt your business or services to new workplace needs? Successful individuals plan with future contingencies in mind.

HELPFUL IDEAS FOR UNCOVERING YOUR PASSION

- Explore opportunities beyond your comfort level.

- Ask family, friends and colleagues for feedback and ideas.

- Set time aside to be still with your thoughts.

- Clarify your core values.

- Read, research and take classes.

- Allow yourself to daydream.

- Visualize the possibilities.

- Write all thoughts and ideas in a journal.

- Surround yourself with people and places that inspire hope.

- Take advantage of the chaos to experiment and explore.

- Try something different to spark creativity—work on a hobby, travel or volunteer.

PASSION VS. RESPONSIBILITY

Many of you grew up with parents, teachers and other mentors who stressed responsibility above personal satisfaction. Unfortunately, most of them went too far, turning you into productive citizens at the expense of the inner joy that plants the seeds of passion in our lives. In many families, artistic pursuits were not valued as viable professional options. "You can't make a living at that!" they'd say. Or, "if it's that much fun, it can't be work." As a result, you learned that being creative was not responsible, and that you would never succeed at such endeavors, regardless of how passionately you felt about them.

Those may not have been the messages your families intended, but they are the ones you created and believed. A negative side effect was that you began to doubt your own personal judgments and desires when choosing a career path. You spent years following other people's advice instead. It's time to take ownership of your thought processes and explore why you place more emphasis on the beliefs and desires of others than on your own.

When you accept someone else's beliefs to be more valid than your own, your life may seem quite satisfying, until you lose your job due to a merger or challenging economy. A job displacement often reveals pent up dissatisfaction and anger at the choices you felt you had to make to meet expectations or maintain a certain lifestyle. You may feel stifled and isolated by the pressure of someone else's ideas about how you should live.

The first step to regain passion in your life is to fully own the decisions, steps and behaviors you have chosen up to this point. Your life is the result of your choices and reactions to events. Some events are, of course, undeserved or out of your control. But there is opportunity in every experience, if you choose to look for it.

Disruption is a gift that forces you out of your familiar, safe, comfort zone. You are able to look within your life and see the sticking points. What thoughts or feelings do you have about these areas in your life? Do they bring you joy? Or, do you feel stymied, stuck, with no options? If you feel you are living according to someone else's standards, you may not even allow yourself to feel that you deserve otherwise. It may not occur to you to doubt the way things ought to be. Moving out of your comfort zone to acknowledge these beliefs and feelings is critical to breaking old mental habits and to identifying your hidden talents and passions.

What about your obligations to other people? Do you sometimes strive to make others happy at the expense of events and relationships you care about? Do you feel constricted by your commitments or the expectations of your families, friends, coworkers or boss? Sometimes it's overwhelming just to get out of bed to face all the responsibilities. If you find yourself feeling or thinking this way, then it is definitely time to rekindle the search for joy and passion in your life. The fallacy is to believe that in fulfilling your own life, you will disappoint others.

When you begin integrating activities or events that bring you joy, other people will notice a change in you. When you are happier, the people around you are happier. They may initially object to or advise against making changes, but when you are joyful and successful, they all want to feel the same way. The reality is that you can be responsible and passionate at the same time. You just have to focus on what is really important to you and satisfy your passion perspective.

Given the enormity of what you may be trying to do, either in response to change from outside or because you realize that you would be happier doing something else, you may be so overwhelmed that you can't focus. This next strategy helps you identify joys, marketable skills and sustainable career elements. Allow ample time to complete this exercise, generally over the course of a week. Write down your initial thoughts and keep updating the exercise as you become more at ease listening to your subconscious self.

TIP #19

USE YOUR POWER CORE FOR SUCCESS

Your Power Core encompasses the skills and traits that uniquely qualify you to succeed. It is composed of four realms of your life: 1) your current skills and talents, 2) activities and relationships that you enjoy, 3) elements that encourage personal motivation in a work environment and 4) the probability of long-lasting success.

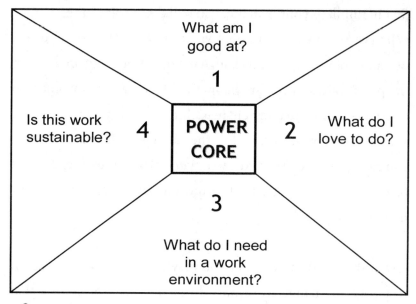

INSTRUCTIONS:

1. **What am I good at?** List all the skills you presently possess. Ask friends and colleagues, review performance appraisals and reflect upon those tasks at work that consume you in a positive way. Look for reoccurring themes. For instance, do you find yourself in work that requires you to be organized or to multitask? Highlight the skills that have common traits in your list. _____

    _____

    _____

2. **What do I love to do?** List any hobbies, escape activities, physical exercises, tasks or events that bring you joy, either at work or at home, as well as joyful personal relationships. If you don't have time for hobbies or recreational activities, ask yourself what you would enjoy if time and money were no object. _____

    _____

    _____

3. **What do I need in a work environment?** List all the elements you find necessary to be productive and successful. These are your core values at work. Do you need interaction with people? Do you like to set your own deadlines? Is freedom to explore your ideas important? Are you more comfortable working alongside your colleagues or supervising them? _____

    _____

    _____

    _____

4. **Is this work sustainable?** List the sustainable elements of your chosen work. Does your research predict the need for your specific skills or industry? If so, for how long? Can these tasks be outsourced? Is there any area of the industry that is not being fully served? What trends do you instinctively believe are important to your work? Where do people find value in what you do? How much are they willing to pay for this work? _____

    _____

    _____

    _____

Once you've completed your power lists, the next step is to analyze your answers for overall themes. What stands out as you review your answers? Are there skills, qualities or ideas that occur in two or more quadrants? If so, list these items in the center Power Core box. What possible industries need your qualifications and interests? Can you create a need for your talents? List these ideas in your Power Core, as well.

The Power Core diagram is a great tool to allow your brain to objectively seek new opportunities and assess your talents and skills. You'll visit this diagram again at the end of the chapter, when it's time to identify and promote your marketable skills.

Case Study – The Power Core in Action

Barbara Glanz has been "Spreading Contagious Enthusiasm™" for almost 25 years. This author, speaker and consultant began her career as a schoolteacher. Despite the loss of her husband, her indomitable spirit and outlook on life propelled her to produce 11 top-selling books on regenerating spirit in the workplace, motivating employees, serving customers and creating positive work atmospheres. Barbara is a living example of the upside.

When you meet Barbara in person, you immediately feel as though you are reconnecting with a long-lost friend. That is Barbara's power core: the ability to put you at ease and inspire you to make the world a better place, one person at a time. Hers is not a new message nor is it unique; however, Barbara embodies this trait to the point where corporations and organizations on all *seven* continents have hired her to help them foster more creative work environments that encourage top performance. She has used her positive outlook and passion to transform everyone she counsels into an incredibly successful businessperson.

Are you an expertise vendor or topic expert?

As new industries, jobs and opportunities emerge, you will need to assess your skills accordingly. Two new trends are on the horizon for creating sustainable skills: expertise vendors and topic experts.

An expertise vendor is someone who can create a demand or market for his particular skill or information. He may cater to a specific group or niche, or be recognized as the go-to person within an industry. When a broad spectrum of individuals and businesses want his products and services, the expertise vendor is poised to become a successful entrepreneur.

A topic expert is also highly qualified and recognized in her field. The difference is that she prefers the structure of an organization, as opposed to branching out on her own. Topic experts excel within a specific set of qualifications and circumstances; they comprise the majority of the American workforce. Many topic experts go on to become influential leaders within their organizations.

It's important to note that just because you have talent, great ideas or excellent rapport with people, you are not necessarily ready to become an expertise vendor or entrepreneur. Even though you may be consumed by your work and topic, to succeed as an expertise vendor you must incorporate and enjoy the skills needed to run an effective business.

UNDERSTANDING YOUR EXPERTISE: CASE STUDY #1
Stephanie recently moved to a new city and was looking for a hairdresser. Seeing a neighbor with an attractive cut, she inquired about the stylist, LeeAnn, and made an appointment. LeeAnn's shop was cluttered and chaotic, but Stephanie wrote it off as part of the creative personality and received an excellent haircut.

Her next appointment did not go as well. Although the haircut was manageable, LeeAnn appeared distracted and talked about the difficulties of running a business. Over the course of a year,

Stephanie's haircuts became more and more erratic, sometimes excellent and other times difficult to style. On her last visit to LeeAnn, she observed that the salon had deteriorated beyond cluttered to unkempt, and was in complete disarray. LeeAnn was notably distracted, couldn't locate her cutting tools, and finally confided that she was considering closing the shop because she couldn't pay her bills. To top it off, the haircut was less than satisfactory and Stephanie vowed not to return.

LeeAnn did close her business and went back to work in a friend's salon. Given a solid environment where she could focus on her skill and craft, LeeAnn excelled. She won several local style competitions and rebuilt a loyal clientele, including Stephanie. The difference is that she no longer had the pressures of running the business. LeeAnn's expertise in her field was outstanding, but she mistook that talent for the ability to successfully own and manage her own salon. The reality was that LeeAnn was not ready to become an expertise vendor. She could, however, flourish as a topic expert, earning a better income because she was now focused on her skills.

UNDERSTANDING YOUR EXPERTISE: CASE STUDY #2

Michael had a good life—nearly 23 years in management with a major supermarket chain allowed him and his wife Daneen to live comfortably. Then, tragedy struck: Michael was seriously injured in a car accident. The resulting neck and back pain was constant. The upside was that it motivated Michael to re-evaluate his life.

His wife shared a dream she had about people wearing T-shirts with the slogan: Make Good Choices. "Making good choices" was the couple's parenting theme while raising their family, and before long, Michael found himself designing artwork that incorporated the same idea. He created a company character named Godwin as a marketing vehicle and sold his "apparel with a positive edge" to local retail shops, churches and online venues.

Michael took a core value from his life and turned it into marketable retail items. He repurposed his business background to organize a profitable structure for the new company. In short, Michael became an expertise vendor by accurately assessing his knowledge and skills, and then translating his passionate message into a sustainable business.

EXPLORING YOUR OWN LEVELS OF EXPERTISE

We'll single out Power Core quadrant #3 for this exercise. Carefully review your responses and look for a connecting thread. Are you most comfortable working in an established environment or do you crave the excitement of calling your own shots? Be brutally honest with yourself and take time with this exercise. You may have grown accustomed to your current situation and mistake that comfort level for your answer.

To start identifying your most productive work environment for quadrant #3, complete the following exercise, including as much detail as possible. In what activities are you active throughout the day? How does this feel? Who is the boss? Who are the clients? What product or service do you provide?

My ideal day at work is: _____

_____

_____

_____

Look at the description you just wrote. How close is it to your real life? Is this fantasy workday attainable? What must you do to achieve this? Begin writing the steps you can take to incorporate the essence of the ideal workday into your present workday.

Look at your scenario again and revisit your idea of who is in charge of your business. Compare this with quadrants 1 and 2. Is there opportunity in your present job or industry to incorporate these qualities? Do you feel rewarded for your work? Where does your greatest satisfaction lie at the end of your workday?

The answers to these questions determine whether you have the mindset to be an expertise vendor or topic expert. Our changing global market needs both, but it is important for you to be clear about your own needs before you can create a sustainable career.

TYING PASSION TO YOUR SUSTAINABLE SKILLS

You've found your passion—something that excites you, a career path, business or job that interests you. Do you have the skills required for the job? What new skills do you need to attain? What existing skills need to be refined or updated?

When Tom began his business, he already possessed skills in training, speaking and writing. To excel and become profitable, Tom recognized that he needed more information about needs assessments, running an actual business and developing a marketing plan, so he joined a business networking group and attended workshops. He also took classes in marketing and researched needs assessments in the marketplace. Exposing himself to new skills gave Tom the courage and confidence to be a successful business owner.

Which comes first, matching your skills to a career path or finding your passion and then developing your skills? There isn't one right or wrong way. Being creative and highlighting skills that are sustainable in the changing workplace are the important factors. Because you are so accustomed to your talents, it can be difficult to envision how your current skills are transferable. Go through the following exercise to define your own transferable skills.

Sustainable skills exercise: "I am successful."
The first step is to identify everything you are currently doing that makes you successful in your job and at home. List all the skills, talents and qualities you have by completing the statement below. You may want to use ideas from Quadrant #1 of the Power Core exercise.

I am successful because: _____

_____

_____

_____

_____

Now that you have a tangible list, consider each quality individually. What is it about each quality that brings a benefit to your employer or customers? For example, let's say you are a good listener. The benefit of being a good listener is that you get information correctly the first time and avoid costly mistakes and rework. Perhaps you are very organized. The benefit of that is that you can locate items or information quickly, reducing the amount of response or down time. Get the idea? List a benefit for each quality, skill or talent you wrote down for this exercise.

The final step is to assess the sustainability of these skills. Perhaps you are proficient with certain software. How long is that software useful before an upgrade change is necessary? What about soft skills? How can being a good listener be sustainable? As a good listener, you may be developing concentration skills that enable you to work in a highly distractible environment. That is certainly a desirable, sustainable component.

PROMOTING YOUR SUSTAINABLE SKILLS

The previous exercise is one of the hardest parts of the marketing equation, although sharing your skills with others can feel much more stressful. Many of us are uncomfortable promoting our great talents; it feels as if we are bragging. Unfortunately, whether you are an expertise vendor or a topic expert, you don't have the luxury of feeling uncomfortable when it comes to promoting yourself. Speak up or perish!

Here's an easy way to talk about yourself or your business. Add a second part to the "I am successful because," sentence with "my area of expertise is," and include a benefit. A sample sentence might sound like this: *As an analyst with the ABC Company, it's my job to save money by comparing costs between competing vendors.* That sounds a lot better than "I oversee ordering supplies."

You can use the same tactic when describing a business. Here are ways to describe a company that transports documents and stores excess inventory:

- *Good:* We save our customers time by providing door-to-door pick-up and delivery.

- *Better:* We save our customers time and money by providing quick, convenient, door-to-door transfer of their internal documents. Another cost-saving option is our in-house storage facility, which saves businesses the expense and legal entanglement of long-term rental contracts offsite.

- *Best:* We provide fast delivery solutions for customer's documents and goods. Our on-site warehouse service eliminates the need for expensive, long-term rental contracts.

INTEGRATING YOUR PASSIONS AND SKILLS INTO THE CHANGING WORKPLACE

You've done your homework and found some careers that excite you. You have analyzed how your skills might be applicable to the chosen careers. Here comes the kicker. How do you know this career path is sustainable? We are coming full circle now. If you want to prosper and succeed, the next step will be the most important. What does the future look like? This entails serious research, rather than looking into a crystal ball. This is where you take on the role of a visionary.

To help you predict the future, begin to expand your knowledge of the local and global economy. Read articles, books and blogs; network with contacts; and take classes. Build support networks and meet with individuals who can help you think objectively—movers, shakers, thinkers and futurists. Let them play devil's advocate and ask the hard questions, in addition to offering suggestions.

KAREN'S STORY

Before Karen started her business, she researched workplace trends, demographics, the changing economy, family needs and current services being offered to corporate human resources. She attended workshops on the aging population and the demographic effect on workplaces. She learned that the workplace was experiencing shortages and more women were being recruited. These women often had children, elders or other family responsibilities. Many human resource departments did not have the necessary services, benefits or programs to support the new needs created when women were hired, and there were few childcare options for working women.

Her research identified one company—IBM—that was incorporating innovative family programs to recruit and retain loyal, productive employees. They were changing their corporate culture to help workers balance work and family. At the time, it was a novel idea. Most companies had not yet recognized the need to provide these programs.

Karen began to connect the dots and asked herself several questions. What services, benefits and programs do companies need to recruit and retain working women? What will companies pay for such services? How would this business need to be marketed? How sustainable is this concept? Based on the statistics, demographics and workplace needs, she concluded that this business enterprise could be sustainable for a long time.

Over the last two decades, Karen's company has evolved and changed as trends, the economy and workplace needs changed. For example, her company expanded internationally by creating a franchise in Australia, after researching workplace trends abroad. Like the United States, Australian businesses were experiencing the same challenges and demands in an upward-bound economy. It was a seamless process to extend similar services and training programs to a quickly growing market.

Whether you are an expertise vendor or a topic expert in a company, you still have to go through the same business development process. A case in point: if you find the ideal job and have the skills, but you haven't evaluated its sustainability, you'll probably end up going through the job search again in the future. Learning to read patterns and anticipate global changes is still critical. If there is no place in the future for your career or job, stop now and move on. Don't hold on to something that will be extinct in the near future.

When doing your research, look to companies and industries that usually survive in an economic downturn, such as health care, cosmetics, food products and entertainment. Why do they survive? What makes them sustainable, even during a recession?

It is, of course, impossible to predict the future, but doing your homework with constant research will give you a stronger chance at success. What do you see in the future? What products, services and skills will be needed? What industries, products or services are at the forefront of new technology and ideas? What jobs, services or business opportunities might be viable for you to explore internationally? The time is now to embrace global changes and look forward to new possibilities.

CHANGING THE PARADIGM

Your assignment now is to integrate your passion with your skills and build your career model on today's realities. These realities may require you to let go of former comforts and expectations when creating your new, customized and sustainable career. You are creating a path and changing old paradigms. Consider the following:

CHANGING THE PARADIGM—BUILDING YOUR CAREER MODEL

- Become a visionary. Look ahead for emerging trends beyond your day-to-day responsibilities.

- Continually research forecasts and trends.

- Develop support networks.

- Accept reality. Don't be in denial over changes in your industry or the economy.

- Look for similarities and connect the dots.

- Attend workshops and conferences.

- Read material out of the mainstream.

- Ask yourself hard questions.

- Integrate passion, sustainability and reality.

CASE STUDY: TARGETING A SPECIFIC MARKET

Jonathon worked for a major publishing company for almost 20 years as a trademark and copyright attorney. The company was purchased by a major media conglomerate, which then opted for its own legal department, so Jonathon found himself unexpectedly unemployed.

Due to family obligations, Jonathon needed to remain in his current city, but was unable to find employment with other firms or organizations during the economic slump. So, he turned to what he knew best: trademark and copyright law. He used innovative thinking skills and decided to create a market that would come to him.

Jonathon began identifying small businesses that could use his services. At a networking event, he met a corporate trainer interested in developing her own series of manuals to sell to other organizations. That contact led him to a group of professional trainers and authors who also needed help acquiring copyright protection for their materials.

Now, Jonathon maintains a flourishing business in trademark law, assisting entrepreneurs, speakers and authors. He works via the Internet and phone, with flexible hours. Best of all, his business is spreading through referrals and in just one year, his income is stable and equal to that in his former corporate life.

A SUSTAINABLE CAREER PARADIGM

Use the worksheet on the following pages to help you identify your sustainable career.

WORKSHEET:
My career model:

Core values

- _____
- _____
- _____
- _____
- _____

Passions

- _____
- _____
- _____
- _____
- _____

Marketable skills

- _____
- _____
- _____
- _____
- _____

Changing workplace considerations

- _____
- _____
- _____
- _____

Possible jobs, careers or businesses

- _____
- _____
- _____
- _____
- _____

SUMMARY

Congratulations! You've embarked on an introspective and invigorating process to create a sustainable professional life. Remember, this process takes time, so allow several weeks to complete the exercises and ideas. Sustainable success is also determined by how well you manage your money, which we'll cover in the next chapter.

REMINDERS

- **Identify core values.**

- **Identify marketable skills.**

- **Uncover your passion.**

- **Research sustainable jobs, industries and new opportunities.**

- **Apply to new economies, targeted industries and emerging markets.**

CHAPTER 6

YOUR PERSONAL PROSPERITY: THE ROLE OF MONEY IN A CHANGING WORLD

Money is really a symbol of the life energy exchange and the life energy we use as a result of the service we provide to the universe.
~ Deepak Chopra, *The Seven Spiritual Laws of Success.*

As the not-known becomes your new reality, your relationship with money is destined to undergo a dramatic change. In this chapter, you will identify your financial beliefs, examine money's emotional impact on your life and clarify the role money plays in your sustainable success. You may decide to reframe your financial paradigm, honoring your true self, instead of following the values of others.

The relationship between money, happiness and success is a pivotal part of an evolving work-life model. Some of you are very talented at making money, only to see it vanish as quickly as it comes; some struggle to create a sense of financial well-being. This chapter will help you initiate a healthy relationship with money. If you are out of work, undergoing financial losses or simply in transition, this is an opportunity to explore the meaning of money for you. Think of this as a time to reassess and make new choices, based on the new reality.

YOUR RELATIONSHIP WITH MONEY

Have you ever stopped to think about the role money plays in your life? Take the time now to reflect on the following questions:

1. Does money make you happy when you have it? _____

2. Does it frustrate or worry you when you don't have it? ____

_____

3. In the past, have you worked longer hours to make more money? _____

4. How much money is enough for you to feel at ease? Can you realistically accomplish that in the new norm or can you exceed that amount? _____

_____

5. Are you in debt now? If so, how did you incur the debt? ___

_____

6. Has money affected the relationship between you and your significant other? Other family members? _____

_____

7. In reviewing the questions above, what insights do you
   have about your relationship to money? _____

   _____

Jerry's story

Jerry was a hard-working, honest and devout man. A father of
four boys, with his first daughter on the way, Jerry attended a
workshop on developing a healthy relationship with money. "I
like money," he proclaimed. "There just needs to be more of it to
go around!"

After completing the questions above, Jerry discovered an
aspect of his financial health he had never considered: he had
set his money "thermostat" at a very low level, one that would
not support his family. Whenever Jerry had an opportunity to
surpass this cap, he choked. Intrigued, he began to reflect upon
why this low financial goal kept occurring and was surprised
when he discovered the source.

Jerry realized that he kept capping his income in order to stay
consistent with the salary his father had earned. Unconsciously,
he believed that if his father could raise a family on that amount,
so should he. He also was concerned that if he made more money
than his father, it might embarrass or discredit his dad. Without
realizing it, Jerry had developed an unhealthy relationship with
financial success.

Do you suspect that you have some hidden factors that impact
or limit your financial flow? Look closely at your answers to
the money relationship questions. What are some of the old,
obsolete thoughts you need to release? Are there expectations
involved? Are you basing these thoughts or expectations on

ideas from your childhood role models or dreams? How can you adjust these thoughts or expectations for the new reality of the not-known?

Money is important to support your daily needs, and the new norm requires you to reevaluate those needs. The question becomes how much money is needed to fulfill your basic needs for food, housing and other essentials. In the 1970s, the average house was 1,700 square feet, with three bedrooms and one-and-a-half baths. Many households now cover more than 3,200 square feet to accommodate large kitchen islands, massive televisions and bedroom suites. Our intent is not to judge, but to ask whether or not this lifestyle is sustainable. Can the new economy support it?

REALITY CHECK: ARE YOU RICH OR POOR?

How much money do you need to feel rich or secure? You'll find that the answer depends on whom you ask, and that the figure changes from year to year, depending upon the economy. Some working-class people think they are middle class and live above their means. Others believe they need multi-million-dollar yearly incomes. If you knew that, according to IRS statistics, your yearly income placed you in the top 10 percent of income earners, would you feel any richer? Would you spend more? How rich you feel could be affecting your spending habits, which in turn, affects your net worth.

For years, Americans have liberally spent their money, accumulated things, and indebted themselves, ultimately creating a false sense of security. When the latest recession began, those same people were shocked. They had no idea how bad the economy was or how financially insecure they actually were.

As economic realities continue to mount, this is a good time to examine past spending habits and reconsider priorities. We all need to take control of our finances. Scrutinize your bills and credit card statements. Study your financial choices and lifestyle. Is there room for adjustment? Are you spending money on cars and homes to impress others, or are you saving your money to attain financial stability?

TIP #20

REPROGRAM YOUR FINANCIAL THERMOSTAT

When it comes to your beliefs about money, many of you are caught in the cycle of unconscious acceptance. This means that you accept popular ideas about money and spending without thinking, even when these ideas are contrary to your core values. This phenomenon is so commonplace that you often fail to see how it undermines your true identity. Rampant advertising has led you to believe that the more money you have, the better your life will be. The lifestyles depicted on television shows and in movies are often unattainable, but you've come to accept them as normal and feel entitled to them, even if you lack the financial means to support them.

> *Money weaves our whole society together, and yet it's amazing how little we know about how to make it work best for us.*
>
> ~ Davis Fisher, money consultant

THE PRESTIGE TRAP: HELEN'S STORY

As a speaker, trainer and executive coach, Helen worked with highly successful individuals. She traveled quite a bit to visit clients; sitting in airports allowed her to study emerging social trends and behaviors. Several years ago, she began noticing women's handbags and was surprised to see how many carried designer purses that cost from several hundred to several thousand dollars. Being the practical sort, Helen didn't spend much on her purses.

Then she began to notice the types of purses her clients were carrying; even the administrative support had designer logos that were triple the cost of her own, and she wondered what message this sent to her high-level customers. Although she charged significant fees for her time and expertise, her apparel did not reflect the perceived designer status.

Helen succumbed to the social pressure and purchased a modest label designer bag. She was surprised by the reactions she received about her handbag, as if she had become the member of a club or private society. She learned first-hand how people judged success externally as a result of unconscious or blind acceptance.

After experiencing this on the receiving end, Helen questioned whether she was susceptible to the same behavior—when taking vacations or purchasing a car, for example. She now carefully weighs her purchasing decisions to determine if they are based on peer pressure or pure desire.

To move beyond this blind acceptance, review the core values you wrote in previous chapters. How do those values correlate with your actual money practices? Are you honoring your true self or are you caught up in values that are promoted by outside sources? Is it a mixture of both? What direction will make your life more sustainable on a day-to-day basis?

Another thought to consider while assessing your financial thermostat is what would happen if your present income were frozen for the next five to 10 years? What changes would you need to make? Can you make more money or increase your income, if needed? If you are counting on a raise from your present employer, you may want to think again. There is a distinct trend against employee raises. If you want to substantially increase your income or salary, chances are you will need to obtain new skills to be promoted or to switch organizations altogether.

TIP #21

DEVELOP CASH CONSCIOUSNESS

The goal of this chapter is for you to become aware of your motivations and habits in acquiring and spending money and then change what won't work under the new norm. Sustainable success requires that you learn from your expectations, mistakes and misconceptions, in order to become flexible and open to new ways of relating to money. If you want a relationship with money that reflects the changing times, you must be honest and willing to look deeper into your behavior.

What does money mean to you? Does it represent security, freedom or comfort? Explain how those descriptions affect your lifestyle choices. For instance, if money means security, you may be more willing to save it. If money means comfort, you may want to accumulate more than is necessary for your basic needs. If you are trying to prove your worth by acquiring money, the happiness or success you seek may prove to be elusive.

What money means to you exercise:

Fill out the following chart and reflect on the outcome and benefits of your definition of money.

Money means:	Outcome	Benefits
Financial freedom	Comfortable retirement	Long-term security, less stress
An anchor, stability	Able to pay bills	Less worry and anxiety

Another important aspect of your relationship with money is to understand how it changes throughout your life. While some people are born with a high financial drive, most of you learn about money and what it can and cannot do for you from an early age. Complete the following exercise to determine what roles money has played in your life.

FINANCIAL DECADES EXERCISE

For each decade of your life, write down the money memories you have, then determine what that example meant at that point.

Age	Memory	Money outcome or belief
0-10		
11-20		
21-30		
31-40		
41-50		
51-60		
61-70		

FINANCIAL DECADES CASE STUDY: JULIA

Age	Money outcome or belief
0-10	The allowances my parents gave me taught me that money must be earned and that you had to work for it. Also had an experience that created an unhappy belief about money: that I could not "keep" my money and still get what I wanted.
11-20	I earned money from babysitting and my first real job in retail. I liked accumulating money for projects. I paid my way to Europe, bought my own clothes, etc.

21-30   On my own, money was more elusive. I did not have enough money to live as I did with my parents. Began using credit cards to provide desired lifestyle, with the belief that I would pay them off later. Was laid off for the first time with no income; qualified for food stamps and learned that I could rebuild wealth. Still not good at holding on to it; tended to accumulate and then spend.

31-40   Married, inherited children, husband and I both get laid off at same time. Realized that I did not have enough money to have my own child. Later built beautiful home and began traveling.

41-50   Sold home, made money in real estate, bought second home to be near parents. Money was still tight, although we lived well. Realized that I was conditioned to live well without saving money. Real estate crisis and husband's lawsuit caused financial strain. Began to understand how low my financial thermostat was set.

FINANCIAL DECADES CASE STUDY: RICHARD

21-30   Did not think much about money specifically, but wanted sufficient earnings to support an independent lifestyle. A modest apartment, some clothes, some local and camping travel. Marriage and children had an impact but lived within means. Career was promoted with additional schooling and various job changes.

31-40   Accumulation of money. Began long-term money connections with purchase of first house. This was coupled with greater expenses for child rearing and concerns about college. Thus, this was a more significant period for making money and attempting to live within means and moderate savings. A dual income household helped in this regard.

41-50   Balance became a priority. Was willing to earn less in exchange for more free time, but was still concerned about investment and savings. College expenses and no longer having a dual income household were factors in achieving goals.

51-60   Security; retirement thinking created greater focus on savings and investment. Goal was sufficiency.

MARTHA'S STORY:

Martha grew up in a socially prominent family in the South. Her family was comfortable, but not wealthy, although many of her parent's friends were. She became comfortable around wealth and grew accustomed to many of the niceties: beautiful homes, travel and club memberships. There was never a question in her mind that she would marry someone who could provide for her in the manner to which she'd become accustomed. The thought of providing for herself did not enter into her plans.

Later in life, Martha was embarrassed to admit that she had such antiquated ideas. She considered herself an equal in her marriage, but this apparently did not include equal financial responsibilities. Martha admitted that this was hardly fair to her family.

Although she was very successful on her own in earlier years, she tended to work for the interest of the job, rather than the financial stability. This caught up with her because her financial thermostat was considerably lower than what she could actually achieve. Many of her friends who started similar businesses at the same time she did were now multimillionaires. What did this tell her? Her relationship with money was not healthy, an eye-opener for someone who appeared successful by all outward appearances.

Nadine's story:

Nadine came from a poor home. They weren't in dire circumstances, but her family always struggled to make ends meet. She didn't know she was poor until she met some new acquaintances in high school and visited their homes. Admittedly, she envied their lifestyles, but she wasn't unhappy because her family provided a loving home with enough food, shelter, clothes and money for music lessons. It seemed to be enough.

As a young adult, she worried somewhat about making enough money to live on, but it didn't take away from her core values. As a single parent, she did have to provide for her daughter, but the goal wasn't to accumulate as much as it was to provide a safety net and some back-up savings.

Through the years, not much has changed with her lifestyle choices of moderate living. There have been ups and downs with careers, losses and gains, yet there is a strong core that has kept her balanced in her relationship with money. For Nadine, the lessons have not been about money, but about career choices, friendships, a good life partner and stimulating activities. She was able to indulge her love of travel, not with lots of money, but by being resourceful.

SPENDING STYLE IMPACTS PROSPERITY

You described your relationship with money in the previous section and the role it played as your life changed. If you had to explain your money style to a good friend, what would you say? Would you describe yourself as a spender, saver or somewhere in-between?

If you are a spender, how does that affect your overall prosperity? When does the need to spend occur most often? What emotional gratification do you feel when spending? In five years, can you guess whether you will still be able to spend the same amount of money you are spending now? Do others resent your spending habits? How does this affect your relationships? How does the new norm impact your spending habits?

If you are a saver, what does that do to your lifestyle? Are you sacrificing meaningful life experiences to satisfy your need to save? Five years from now, can you still save the same amount of money you are saving now? Do others resent your ability to save? How does this impact your relationships? Will the new norm require you to adjust your savings?

To create sustainable success, you must adapt in order to prosper. In your search for answers regarding your relationship to money, you are better served if you understand that prosperity is a state of mind that can help you to attain true wealth and happiness in life.

To help you clarify your focus, write down what prosperity means to you. Can you name individuals who have achieved the prosperity mindset? What qualities do they possess? What can you learn from them?

Prosperity for me is: _____

_____

_____

_____

_____

As you review your definition, decide if it is compatible with your family, spouse or significant other. How might this agreement or disagreement impact your mindset, goals or relationship?

Your prosperity quotient

Complete the following exercise to better understand your outlook on money and your overall prosperity. The goal here is to help you analyze your fiscal thought process and how it affects your overall well-being.

Check all of the statements in the following chart that are true for you:

	Column A	Column B	
	I am fully responsible for all that happens in my life.	If others are successful, that means there is less for me.	
	I have clear goals and intentions about what is important in my life.	What happens in the rest of the world has nothing to do with me.	
	I have a solid sense of self-esteem.	Circumstances beyond my control shape my life.	
	I am a creative and resourceful problem solver.	It makes me uncomfortable when people compliment me or my work.	

	I am aware of the changing influences in my life, work and family.	I have difficulty asking for help.	
	I believe there is plenty of abundance for all.	I feel stagnant or stuck in the life process.	
	It is easy for me to accept help and support from others.	I feel frustrated by a lack of direction in achieving what I want in life.	
	I am gracious in receiving gifts and compliments from others.	I feel guilty if I spend money on myself.	
	I am fully engaged in the life process.	I don't mind working in a job I don't like if it pays well.	
	It's okay to invest in myself financially to improve my success.	I tend to procrastinate on projects or tasks that are not fun or are too hard.	
TOTAL A			TOTAL B

Add up the number of responses for both columns. Which column has the most responses? If Column A is the highest, you are well on your way to living a prosperous mindset. If Column B is the highest, you are prone to scarcity thinking, which is defined by the belief that there is not enough abundance in the world for everyone to be prosperous.

Notice that you have check marks in both columns. While your desire to develop a prosperous mindset is reflected in column A, it's natural to have doubts or barriers based on past experiences, as shown in column B. Pay close attention to your answers marked in the B column, they can indicate new areas in which to grow your comfort zone to overcome these subtle, but significant barriers.

The most important step lies ahead: now that you've defined prosperity and have an insight into your fiscal thinking process, it's time to start creating a plan for your new sustainable lifestyle.

CLARIFYING NEED VS. WANT

"I need that toy!" exclaims a child to his mother in a store. This often-heard phrase is a reminder of our society's use of the word need. We need shelter and food—but what else do we really need? Abraham Maslow created a diagram in 1943 that outlines the basic needs of mankind. Shelter and food are the essential foundation of the hierarchy, and once those are satisfied, love, acceptance, meaningful work and social relationships follow.

While you probably agree with the basics, are you like most people when it comes to thinking about what you need? Most people identify wants as needs, as in Helen's handbag story. She believed she needed the designer handbag to fit in and provide the right image for her client base. In actuality, the bag was a want, a nice-to-have, instead of a need-to-have.

What do you really need vs. want? Complete the following activity to help you determine your need vs. want quotient. Make a list below of things or necessities that you *really* need in your life—items that are a must to exist daily. For instance, can you take public transportation to work? If not, then the necessity of a car is a true need, not a want. Next, evaluate the financial aspect of owning your car. If it's not feasible financially, what are your other options? In this example, carpooling or a car sharing service may be an option to manage the financial burden of maintaining a car full-time.

NEED VS. WANT WORKSHEET:

Complete the following exercise by making a list of everything you need to live comfortably. Then evaluate whether your current financial state supports this list.

Necessity	Need?	Want?	Doable?	Options
Car	X		Expensive to maintain	Carpool or car share

Review this list carefully. Are these items or activities possible to achieve in the new economic reality? What items do you think you need, but really see now that you don't?

This list is harder to make because these necessities are based on your perception of past or current needs, rather than those redefined by the new norm. Remember that the new norm includes a more fluid, simpler lifestyle. What new mindset and habits do you need to develop to live within your means and in the new norm? Revisit the car example above. The old norm is that everyone needs their own personal vehicle. The new norm may not support that, which will require finding an affordable approach to transportation that incorporates sharing costs and cars. Your mindset shifts from the personal status of owning a car to the freedom of low-maintenance transportation options.

The final activity in this section is a financial assessment of all your basic needs related to current income. This exercise will help you determine whether or not you are able to sustain your current method of handling your money.

FINANCIAL ASSESSMENT SHEET

Answer all questions on this form. While many are personal in nature, the more specific you are, the easier it will be to evaluate your situation. Write N/A if an item does not apply.

GROSS MONTHLY INCOME	
Source	Amount
Employment income	
Overtime bonus, commission	
Public assistance (food stamps, welfare, unemployment)	
Rental income	
Other (alimony, child support, investments, bonds, interest)	
No current income	

MONTHLY EXPENSES

Be as specific as possible.

Type	Comments/ Details	Monthly amount	Remaining amount owed
Rent			
Mortgage			
Auto			
Interest expense: Home, car, other			
Taxes			
Loans personal, other			
Utilities: heating			
Utilities: electric			
Utilities: phone			
Credit cards, with monthly payments			
Interest			
Childcare			
Food costs/ dining out			
Entertainment			
Commute expenses (gas, parking, transit)			
Medical			
Discretionary personal expenses			
Vacation			
Gifts/holiday			
Insurance			

ASSETS

Type	Comments/Details	Value
Bank accounts		
Trust funds/ stocks/bonds		
Real estate		
Life insurance		
Cash		
Credit union		
Automobile		
Sale of personal items		
Other		

What have you learned from this exercise? Are you dealing with the reality of your income/outgo status? How do your debts relate to your income level in the present or future? What do you need to adjust or change, given the new norm? For example, if your home is in arrears, consider how to adjust your situation.

EASY CREDIT

The country currently is experiencing the highest mortgage defaults and delinquency rates in the history of the credit card business, as well as the largest amount of outstanding personal debt. Credit cards make it very easy to spend beyond what one can afford. Every choice you make in your life—where to live, eat, play or travel—should be based on real income, not credit. Think cash. Now you can come up with concrete solutions that promote sustainable money management. Otherwise, the chaos will continue and clarity will never be achieved.

If you are in debt now because of credit cards and other short-term borrowing, start by adding up all your monthly interest expense for one year on each of your credit cards. Now look at the total. What could that money do if it wasn't being used to pay off debt? What else would you do if this debt were paid? Make an extra mortgage payment? Take a vacation? Looking ahead, what new habits need to be implemented to manage your credit card debt?

Using credit cards can be an addiction. It's easy to become accustomed to a lifestyle that cannot be supported, and stopping yourself from using cards may be as difficult as it is to stop any other addiction. They are convenient tools when the balance is paid in full every month, and many credit cards provide rewards programs that can save money in the long run. Monitor your credit use carefully to maintain control.

Keep in mind when creating your financial plan that it is important to include activities that are fun, inspirational and meaningful. This doesn't necessarily mean that you have to spend a lot of money.

RESOURCEFULNESS: GETTING WHAT YOU WANT WITHOUT SPENDING A LOT

It's been said that necessity is the mother of invention. If that is true, then the gift of the not-known is creativity. Being resourceful and learning to repurpose are imperative skills for sustainable success. There are many options for you to live the good life without paying in full for them. Your job is to get creative and do a little research to find alternative ways to meet your needs in an affordable manner.

Here are some simple ideas to begin your creative process. Betty's desire for travel, for example, was fulfilled with a little ingenuity. She and her husband exchanged vacation homes and cars with a couple from France. They used their frequent flyer miles for the airline tickets and enjoyed a wonderful month's vacation for very little cash.

Home exchanges are one way to travel without the expense of a hotel. Another method is to volunteer services in exchange for room and board. Or, if you have friends or family in different cities, ask if you can stay a few days. Just be sure to cook a meal or treat them to dinner in exchange for the free rent!

Another method is repurposing. Paula is prone to instigating home improvement projects and is known for reincarnating items around the house. While remodeling her bathroom, she repurposed the cabinets to create a custom work center in the garage. She and her husband installed new countertops and knobs, and then painted the garage floor. When they sold their house, the new owners commented that the upscale workstation in the garage was one of their favorite parts of the house.

Don't forget the time-honored tradition of trading talents and services with friends. Offer to host movie nights for your neighbor's children to give the parents a night out, with the understanding that your neighbor reciprocate the following week. Pair up with a friend to clean out your garage, and then attack their closet. The idea here is to gain support at minimal cost, while you both benefit in the process.

WISH LIST ACTIVITY

Use the following worksheet to make a list of things that you would like to have or do, but can't afford. Then go down the list and begin to formulate ways you might be able to use creative methods to attain them. Use a support group or family and friends to brainstorm with you.

WISH LIST WORKSHEET:

Item, goal or wish	What's needed: money, time, etc.	Obstacles	Strategies and support

PROSPERITY AND AUTHENTICITY

Making money work for you in the new norm requires a holistic approach—one that includes the new economic reality, job opportunities and your core values. When you aren't in debt, you have more freedom to make other choices in your personal life and career.

An approach to prosperity that honors your true self requires that you look inward. In previous chapters you identified a more reality-driven model for holistic success. Your financial goals should match your new career and personal life goals and models. The upside of the new norm is that you are working towards lasting happiness and prosperity, instead of short-term outcomes or quick fixes.

REMINDERS

- **Define your relationship with money.**

- **Reprogram your financial thermostat.**

- **Define prosperity.**

- **Evaluate the meaning of money to you throughout the decades.**

- **Distinguish between want vs. need.**

- **Analyze your income and money outflow.**

- **Reevaluate your credit card habits.**

- **Determine ways to be more resourceful.**

CHAPTER 7

THE SUSTAINABLE SOUL: REDEFINING YOUR INNER LIFE IN A CHANGING WORLD

And in all of my experience, I've never seen lasting solutions to problems, lasting happiness and success that came from the outside in.

~ Stephen Covey

By now, you have a fairly accurate picture of your desires, talents, lifestyle choices and monetary needs. You understand that life is undergoing a dramatic change as the not-known becomes a daily reality. It's time to focus on the most powerful part of you: your inner core, or soul. Soul is used in many contexts; we define it as the vital energy of who you are. It combines your beliefs, personality and core values; it is the life force of your being. Your soul is unique.

Because your soul is at the vibrant heart of your being, it would be inadvisable to focus on only the external factors of your life and not acknowledge the inner factors. A nurtured soul is strong and resilient; a suffering soul is stagnant and depressed. Your soul is the root of your life, and just like any plant, needs nurturing and attention in order to flourish. This chapter will give you insight into staying focused and anchored in a constantly changing world. The idea is to live a more authentic life with intention, purpose and creativity, ultimately helping you design and sustain a new work and life paradigm.

TIP #22

MASTER MINDFULNESS

Have you ever driven home and not remembered pulling into your driveway, or left the house and wondered if you turned off the coffee maker? When you engage in routine activities, your mind switches to an unconscious or autopilot mode. Although your body is going through the motions, your mind is engaged elsewhere; you filter out what is happening at the present moment. You see examples of this all the time: missing your turn in traffic, walking into a room and forgetting why you went there or forgetting your sister-in-law's name. While there are times when autopilot comes in handy—for brushing your teeth—living on autopilot robs your life of joy and causes you to miss moments that can never be relived. Because your mind is occupied elsewhere, you lose the ability to engage the world around you.

> *The mind is everything; what you think, you become.*
> ~ Gautama Buddha

The solution to an autopilot existence can be summed up in a single word: mindfulness. Living in the present moment—being mindful—is much harder and takes more energy than letting your mind stray to the past or future. It requires deep, direct awareness of everything going on around you at that moment. Mindfulness brings clarity and allows your focus to stay on track. The benefits of mindfulness include peace of mind, enhanced communication abilities, clarity of thought, reduction of stress, confidence and resilience. It will help you recognize and evaluate your options as you develop your sustainable life plan.

Constant interruptions, distractions and multi-tasking can compromise your mindfulness. Our multi-focused society has created a concentration crisis in your head. Although your inner self craves mindfulness, your brain is conditioned to seek constant activity. Common culprits are e-mails and social media endeavors.

The reality is that technology is here to stay. Society's rampant use of it, however, can blur the boundaries between your personal and professional lives to the point where you feel you are on call 24/7. The question becomes how to make technology work for you, rather than letting it control your life. Real change does not happen while texting. To achieve success in the midst of chaos, you must commit time to be mindful every day. The exercise below can help you create the habit of mindfulness.

BENEFITS OF MINDFULNESS

- Improved focus, concentration and precision
- Enhanced quality of communication and relationships
- Heightened clarity of your thinking and intentions
- Improved efficiency and safety
- Greater peace of mind and sense of flow
- Mastery of stress
- Insight and enhanced intuitive wisdom
- More authenticity in your life work
- Change resilience
- Greater confidence, faith and inner strength

Joel and Michele Levey,
Living in Balance,

MINDFULNESS EXERCISE

Conscious breathing is one simple exercise to strengthen your mindfulness. Sit quietly in your home or office. As you breathe in and out, notice the patterns of your breath. Stay focused and release any thoughts that cross your mind. Relax, and don't try to control your breathing. Begin the activity for three to five minutes, increasing your time as you get better at it. You can do this exercise anywhere, at any time of the day and night. Try it before you tackle an important task or critical thinking project.

MINDFULNESS AND SELF-MASTERY

Mindfulness leads you to the powerful tool of self-mastery, the ability to be self-aware and clear about what you want. It is a state of empowerment that comes when you align yourself with your core values and priorities. Self-mastery takes courage and an ongoing commitment to stay focused and to not succumb to blind acceptance; it is a process that can be integrated into your daily life.

Patricia Varley, life coach and author, uses this example to illustrate self-mastery. "Imagine a raging hurricane, wreaking havoc and devastation all around it. Now, envision the calm eye in the center of the storm. You have just pictured the essence of self-mastery. Although the new norm may be creating chaos around you, the eye of the storm is calm and peaceful."

According to Varley, "in times of stress, rapid change and uncertainty, the power to stay healthy, calm, focused and moving forward is challenged to the max." Whether you are single, moving into retirement, a professional, making a job change, dealing with health issues, a working or stay-at-home mother, recently widowed or divorced, relocating or whatever the circumstances of your life are, self-mastery is an important and necessary component to navigate through these times of personal and professional change.

Varley adds that mindfulness allows you to access your inner commitment and gives you the courage to see yourself and your life from the inside out. By developing success from the inside out, you are connecting with your authentic self, as well as your creative gifts and talents, fortifying your focus and resilience. Helen Harkness, career coach and author of *Capitalizing on Career Chaos*, emphasizes that a successful career can't be based only on what the current marketplace will buy. "To be successful and significant, there must be a shift in identity to that of our authentic self and the discovery of unused parts of ourselves."

To stay mindful throughout the day and be connected with your authentic self, Varley recommends creating a life-purpose statement.

CREATE A GPS LIFE PURPOSE STATEMENT

This exercise is designed to promote the process of self-awareness and authenticity. Varley describes your life purpose statement as your GPS, or Greater Purpose Statement, to help navigate through your life. It is a deeper vision and foundation upon which you build your life and work; in essence, the bigger picture of your life's direction.

List the most satisfying experiences in your life, highlighting those that carry special meaning. Split the experiences into two categories: personal and professional.

WORKSHEET:

The five most satisfying personal experiences in my life are:

1. _____

2. _____

3. _____

4. _____

5. _____

The five most satisfying professional experiences in my life are:

1. _____

2. _____

3. _____

4. _____

5. _____

Was it easier to identify memories in one category or the other? What do you think this means about your life? What significance does this have? _____

_____

_____

What caused these experiences to have deeper or special meaning? _____

_____

_____

Who or what was present that made this event significant?

_____

_____

How does this experience or event continue to impact or shape your life? _____

_____

_____

Review these significant experiences again; they can become the building blocks for your professional and personal goals. For example, Jason found climbing in Nepal to be one of his most satisfying life experiences, because of the physical challenge, combined with the awe-inspiring beauty and cultural differences of the region. His goal now is to incorporate more challenges into his daily routine to stimulate his creativity. Jason found that pushing himself with physical or mental challenges allowed him to see more opportunity in everyday events.

How can you recreate these experiences? What is involved? Does the not-known allow you to recreate them or do you need to adjust? For example, while attending one of the author's conferences on sustainable work-life choices, Stephanie decided that parasailing over the ocean was one of her most satisfying experiences. She loved the freedom of the open sky and felt weightless without the burdens of her everyday responsibilities. When asked how to incorporate that feeling into her present life, Stephanie chose to embrace the not-known as the open sky. Instead of fearing the rapid changes and unclear path, she now found excitement in new options and unexplored opportunities. Stephanie's breakthrough came when she recognized that becoming an expertise vendor would be a better choice for her sustainable success, because it included the freedom and flexibility she craved.

Using the elements of what made these experiences so special, create your own life-purpose statement: _____

_____

_____

_____

EXAMPLES:

"My purpose is to help people solve their problems."

"My mission is to raise my children to make responsible choices."

"I am a guest of my world and environment; my job is to create an awareness of the fragility of our resources."

This exercise can be used as a navigational tool and revised as needed, on an annual basis or as often as you like, to stay on purpose in your life. Post your personal GPS in places where you can see it and reinforce it daily. These statements can become anchors for you in times of chaos.

> ## TIP #23

TAKE TIME OUT TO REFLECT

In order to practice self-mastery and be mindful, you will need
time. Changing your work-life paradigm requires that you take
time for deep reflection, in order to determine
how you want to work and live. Some of you
may be forced into a "time out" because of job
loss. Consider it a blessing in disguise. Embrace
the time and use it well. You may never get the
opportunity to plan out your future again. If
you are currently working full- or part-time, you will have to
discipline yourself to carve out the time. The American way of
life leads you to believe that doing nothing is a bad thing. "Don't
waste your time," is commonly heard. It suggests that value is
only found by being productive or busy every moment.

> *Time is the awareness*
> *of space between events.*
> *~ Jonathan Rowe,*
> *Take Back Your Time*

Jonathan Rowe, writer, thinker and board member of *Take Back
Your Time*, writes that "Time is not infinite, just as air and water
are not. It can be depleted if not husbanded with care. Nor is
time wasted, just because it does not go to market use. Time is
the basic human resource. It is the starting point of freedom. To
choose to use time for more worthy and important ends could
be the next great freedom movement."

Inspiration for making change doesn't come on demand, but
by allowing time to pass without activity. Sometimes you will
be inspired when you least expect it, or when you feel bored.
According to Steven Barrie-Anthony in a 2006 *LA Times* article,
Time out of mind, "Time, with moments of boredom, is the font
from which inspiration emerges and various spiritual traditions
seek to invoke just this timeless sense of being."

Imagine taking a time out for a year! When Betty and Michael took a year-long sabbatical, they had more time than they anticipated. Their underlying goal was to reflect on their lives and determine new priorities and career opportunities. At first, having time without responsibilities and schedules was frightening, but after a period of adjustment, they began to enjoy the luxury of letting time pass without planned activities.

Eventually, they incorporated more structure into their day by adding classes and volunteering, but they still made choices about how to spend their time. Unplanned time, even waiting for buses, trains and planes, had its rewards. The year-long journey gave them new insights on their personal goals, careers, relationship and ideas for simplifying their lifestyles. It was a true renewal experience.

Michael recalls: "One of our renewal goals was to become more authentic, by sharpening our self-awareness and making nurturing choices every day. It was important to take time out for reflection and to simply try some things. The challenge was to stay on the path of self-awareness."

If your schedule won't accommodate a long sabbatical, consider time out in smaller increments; even five to 10 minutes a day can make a surprising difference. Small changes over time make a big impact. Just five minutes a day of quiet or inspirational time over the course of a year equals 3.8 eight-hour business days; 10 minutes takes it to 7.6 days. How would your life be different if you invested more than a week to developing a clear focus through thinking?

Desiring time out is one thing, but finding the time and following through is a challenge. Even if you are out of work, you have many other responsibilities—children, parents, household chores, finding a job, taking classes, and more. If you have a free moment, the easy thing is to go to your computer, iPod or TV to pass some time. Those activities are popular, but unless you schedule time out in your week, it probably won't happen. Think of time that allows for unplanned activities or time to do nothing—sit and watch a sunset, take a walk or meditate.

Getting used to time out can be emotionally unsettling. It is not unusual to feel anxious, sad or depressed when you initially take time to be quiet and reflect. This is simply your body's release of the busy-ness of your life, and these feelings fade each time you practice your quiet time. Releasing these emotions is crucial to your own healing process, so try to welcome them and see them as a step toward clarity and confirmation.

APPLYING SKILLS TO THE WORK-LIFE MODEL

Being mindful is about being aware, not necessarily clearing your mind or having a sense of peacefulness. Being mindful is being conscious of your choices, options and actions and making a deliberate effort to focus on them. It involves taking time out to reflect and redirect, so that you create a life that is meaningful for the long-term. Remember to use these skills not just for planning and direction, but also for times of confusion and frustration. Being mindful is a process; you can't change your life on demand or overnight.

> *The future depends on what we do in the present.*
> ~ Mahatma Gandhi

REMINDERS

- **Nurture your soul to flourish.**

- **Practice mindfulness.**

- **Use mindfulness to strengthen self-mastery.**

- **Create and use a Life Purpose Statement.**

- **Take time out to reflect.**

- **Apply skills to your work-life model.**

CHAPTER 8

LIFESTYLE PROSPERITY: SURVIVING AND THRIVING IN THE NEW NORM

Live full in the here and now. Appreciate the simple things in life. Take responsibility for your destiny.

~ Derek Lin, *The Tao of Daily Life*

Now that you have considered how the not-known and new norm impact your professional and financial life, it's time to explore how these transitions and losses impact your personal life. If you had been warned about the loss you are presently experiencing, would you have made any different decisions? Most of us would have. The goal of this chapter is to generate a sustainable lifestyle that is within your financial means, yet rich in satisfaction, joy and happiness—a prosperous life that is not tied to financial gains yet accommodates unexpected turns of events, losses and an occasional storm.

In redesigning your lifestyle plan, consider the role of your daily life choices and how sustainable they are. You've heard the old adage that every action has a reaction. In this case, every decision has an impact that is either sustainable or not. These choices will either propel you into a more prosperous life or set you back.

In the past, you may have believed that your actions and decisions were independent and isolated, but in reality, peoples' actions are connected. Your lifestyle choices will ebb and flow depending upon global events, economic indicators, climate change and the availability of natural resources. Not unlike the concept of "Six Degrees of Separation," our lives are becoming more connected; what happens around the globe can impact your life within hours.

In a much broader sense of sustainability, we must consider the role that the worlds' changing climate and energy resources play in your future. Remember when oil and gasoline prices went through the roof? This event revealed an ugly reality for many people who could no longer afford to drive their large cars or keep long commutes. We can no longer ignore these realities.

> **Life·style:** *the way a person or groups of people live, including the place they live in, the things they own, the kind of job they do, and the activities they enjoy.*
> ~ Merriam-Webster's dictionary

As you plan ahead for a sustainable future, the idea is to fashion a lifestyle that is not determined solely by your income. In the past, income was the most common way to measure the quality of a lifestyle. Under the new norm, your compensation for work shifts from exclusively monetary and tangible rewards to include emotional and intangible ones as well. Time, freedom, and financial and personal energy management are new defined commodities that can contribute to your sustainable success. The upside of these new currencies is that you are no longer tied to income-driven activities and can incorporate new payoffs into your whole-life plan.

> ## TIP #24

GET A GRIP ON YOUR LIFE

To begin analyzing your personal life choices for long-term success, review the exercises you completed in previous chapters using the checklist below. You've already done the heavy lifting; this is an excellent reminder of the choices you made regarding your career, financial and success models. The goal is to integrate these choices and models into your personal life plan.

LIFESTYLE MODEL PREPARATION CHECKLIST

- ☐ Review your present circumstances, such as job situation, financial and personal issues, etc. Have they changed since you listed them in Chapter 2?

- ☐ Revisit your core values from Chapters 1 and 2.

- ☐ What fears or concerns did you identify in Chapter 3? Have they changed?

- ☐ Review your potential career opportunities from Chapter 5 that are sustainable—industries, jobs, businesses that have the possibilities to last over time.

- ☐ Readdress the personal choices activity in Chapter 2.

- ☐ Review relationship to money activities in Chapter 6.

Here are three more factors that are related to your current lifestyle choices:

1. Describe your idea of a sustainable life. _____

   _____

   _____

2. How do your core values synchronize with your current lifestyle? _____

   _____

   _____

3. List current trends in the economy and other factors that could affect the success of your work life plan. _____

   _____

   _____

Your answers to all of these questions are shaping your new lifestyle model. As you review them, do any patterns or ideas emerge? Keep this in mind as you move to the next stage: designing your new model.

MY CURRENT LIFESTYLE EXERCISE

The purpose of the next activity is to provide you with a realistic picture of how you are currently living. The goal is to help you identify which choices are helping you to live a sustainable life and which are barriers. You may be tempted to skip this process, but doing so puts you at risk of sabotaging yourself and ending up back where you started. For example, if you find a job that provides for your basic needs, but your personal lifestyle choices are not in sync with your salary, you risk sliding down the slippery slope of living beyond your means, incurring unmanageable debt and ultimately, failure.

Current Lifestyle Choices Worksheet:

Write down your current lifestyle choices in the following categories:

- Housing
- Transportation
- Food
- Leisure activities
- Consumer habits

Use descriptive words that help you reflect on the positive or negative aspects. What saves you money or time? Which choices cause you stress or uncertainty? _____

_____

_____

_____

_____

_____

_____

_____

_____

Example #1:

I choose to live in a two-bedroom condo, located in an area with accessible transportation and walking access to a variety of time- and gas-saving destinations. I get to work using public transportation, which saves money. I can walk to grocery stores, the post office, library and leisure activities, which saves gas and stress from driving in traffic. The condo is well insulated and positioned—sun in the winter and shade from trees in the summer. There is a cross-breeze that cools the house and saves on air conditioning. The utilities are low. Water shortages are a concern, so we have installed equipment to monitor our water flow. We run a dishwasher on low and only use it when it is full. This saves on energy. Because dryers use a great deal of energy, we use it sparingly. Living in a warm climate allows us to hang items such as towels outside to dry. We have several local farmers markets and take advantage of seasonal foods. We cook most of the time and save up for a special night out in a restaurant.

EXAMPLE #2:

I live in a multi-story home that requires dual air conditioning systems on a very large lot. Because there is little shade and the house is fully bricked, our utilities run above average. We installed ceiling fans and keep the thermostat comfortably high to combat the expense. The yard work is both time-consuming and a large budget item. Our home is located within an excellent school system where the children can walk to school, but shopping and other activities require personal transportation. The neighborhood is cohesive and hosts many community sponsored events, with a town center for convenient recreation and exercise options.

Once you've written your description, review it closely to determine which lifestyle choices are currently working and which ones need adjustment.

EXAMPLE:

Positive	Needs Improvement
Efficient AC systems	Oversized home with no shade
Affordable neighborhood activities	Lack of alternative transportation
Convenient school system	Costly landscape upkeep
Walk to work	Multiple stories are physically challenging as we age

TWO PRONGS MAKE A RIGHT: INTEGRATE SUSTAINABILITY INTO YOUR LIFESTYLE

Now that you have a better understanding of your current situation, use both short term and long term goals to begin integrating sustainability principles into your lifestyle. Create a proactive personal life plan that incorporates steps you can take now to adjust, plus what you need to do in the next one to two years for the long term.

The short term is often the most stressful to address, so let's tackle it first. What are steps you can take in the next 30-60-90 days to enhance your sustainability? One strategy is to take more time to make conscious choices instead of impulsive ones.

CASE STUDY: A FAMILY OF FOUR

Jake and Isabella rarely gave a second thought to buying items for themselves and their two children, including new laptop computers, toys, expensive sneakers and more. When the recession slashed their income in half, shopping sprees became luxuries and their priorities shifted from products to activities. Now, after school and on weekends, the family explores the local waterways on a secondhand canoe. "I'm trying to teach the kids that you don't necessarily need to spend money or have expensive toys to have fun," says Jake.

Short-term sustainability is achievable when you make affordable, common sense choices every day about what to eat or buy, and how to recreate or socialize. The upside is that it is relatively easy to modify your choices to fit changing needs. As you plan for the next 30-60-90 days, what new-reality currencies will you spend to better balance your whole-life plan?

TIME AFFECTS YOUR LIFESTYLE CHOICES

Individuals who are time-stressed and don't have enough time in the day to change their consumption habits can end up making choices that aren't good for them and their families. As an example, if they had the time, they might choose to prepare healthy, home-cooked foods instead of high-caloric fast foods. While prepared foods are quick and convenient, they often lack balanced nutrition and can be a factor in obesity. Time deficiency can contribute to habits that inhibit your sustainability simply because your time and energy are consumed by other events.

> *In order to seek one's own direction, one must simplify the mechanics of ordinary, everyday life.*
>
> ~ Plato

How do you spend your free time? Are you busy managing people and things in your home life? Do you have time on the weekends to participate in enriching activities and spend time with loved ones, or do you only have time for chores? If your personal life is so over-scheduled that you cannot relax and spend it with friends and family, perhaps you need to make some changes.

How do time management, overwork and over-scheduling affect your lifestyle choices? What are some of the choices you would make differently if time allowed? _____

_____

_____

_____

_____

_____

The issue of time management is not easily solved, but your awareness of the way it affects your choices is an important beginning for making change.

TIME AND CHOICES CHECKLIST

Here are a few helpful tips for you to review.

- ❏ Where does your time go? Keep a log of where you spend your time.

- ❏ Clarify your priorities. What can you realistically change?

- ❏ Choose work that allows you a shorter commute time or negotiate work hours to avoid peak traffic.

- ❏ Limit children's activities to meaningful experiences— don't over-schedule.

- ❏ Visualize how you want to create a life that doesn't have to be filled with activity every minute.

- ❏ Choose work that allows flexibility, vacation and sabbaticals, if possible.

TIP #26

BUILD YOUR BANK ACCOUNT BY UTILIZING SIMPLICITY

Simplicity is a popular concept that millions of people are embracing in many aspects of their lives. Have you considered incorporating simplicity as a day-to-day practice? Simplicity allows you to enjoy a fulfilling life without the burdens of trying to maintain a lifestyle you no longer desire or can afford. It is also a way of life that can promote a healthier and more sustainable environment, which positively impacts you and later generations.

> *Simpler living can often mean more abundant living. To have all we want is said to be rich; but to be able to do without all that we desire is to enjoy true freedom.*
>
> ~ David E. Shi

Living simply isn't living a life of destitution, but one of rearranging priorities.

Identify what is obsolete in your space, schedule or behavior and habits, and then ask, "If this were gone tomorrow, what would I miss?" Stagnant areas of our lives represent a part of ourselves we have put on hold. Once the emotional belief or attachment to an object or practice is discovered, then we can detach from or release it, freeing up space and energy.

Julie Morgenstern's story

Julie Morgenstern, New Times best-selling author of *SHED Your Stuff & Change Your Life: A Four-Step Guide to Getting Unstuck*, tells her story of downsizing to a smaller apartment after her daughter moved out to attend school. Some items were easy to discard, but others presented emotional barriers. While cleaning out her kitchen, Morgenstern was immobilized by a shelf of cookbooks. She became stuck and could not decide what to do with them. After talking it through with a close friend, she realized that these books represented her goal of being a good mother. She had purchased the cookbooks hoping that she would become the type of mother that prepared home-cooked meals for her daughter and friends. Instead, as a single parent, Morgenstern opted for take-out and spent time with her daughter reading and discussing books after dinner. Once she had acknowledged that the opportunity to prepare home-cooked meals for her daughter had passed, only then could she release her attachment to the cookbooks.

Morgenstern notes that the upside of this process is tremendous confidence and the ability to reconnect with your true self.

"When you detach your identity from your possessions, you are able to say, 'I am who I am,' without labeling who you are through belongings."

Embarking on a life of simplicity involves clear intention. You must make deliberate choices from your personal core values, based on what you feel is inherently important and affordable. An upside of wanting less is that in doing so, we create space for the things that really matter.

CASE STUDY: A FAMILY THAT GAVE UP THEIR HOUSE

In Atlanta, the Salwen family combined simplicity and philanthropy in an extraordinary manner. Challenged by their teenage daughter to sincerely make a difference in the world, they decided to sell their house, buy another one half its size and price, and then donate the difference to charity. While that may seem extreme, Kevin Salwen said that living in their dream house, a three-story historic home, did not bring all the joys they had anticipated. While they loved their home, "Our sense of togetherness began to go away. In the big dream house, we scattered in different directions."

> Simplicity creates the opportunity for greater fulfillment in work, meaningful connection with others, feelings of kinship with all life and awe of a living universe. Simplicity involves not only clearing out the physical and emotional clutter and replenishing them mindfully, but also clarifies our view of how our actions have a wider impact.
>
> ~ Duane Elgin

Over the course of a year, the Salwens engaged as a family to research ways to donate their home's proceeds. Eventually, an organization was chosen and the family traveled to meet the villagers their donation would support.

The upside of this process is that they defined their core values as a family, while getting reacquainted with each other as individuals. Today, the Salwens have adjusted to living in half the space and don't miss their previous lifestyle. Sacrifices and adjustments were made, but the Salwens found that, "The more we shared, the more we laughed, teased and bonded." They chronicled their journey in *The Power of Half.*

Another critical upside of simplicity is the financial freedom to make choices that are in sync with your core values. Cecile Andrews, consultant and author of *Less is More,* believes that you can create a life that is happy, healthy and respectful of the planet. Her core values include freedom and love of nature. When evaluating potential career opportunities, her priority was finding a job that she loved and gave her freedom and flexibility. If the job was hardwired with scheduling and all about making money, she didn't pursue it. However, in making these career decisions, Andrews had to reevaluate and adjust her lifestyle so that it was within her financial means. Making conscious choices and exploring alternative lifestyles became an integral part of her core values, and led her to live a simpler lifestyle. "It takes courage, but the examined life, for the well-being of your health, happiness and the planet, is worth it," says Andrews. Her values have also led to a career that includes working with community groups to explore the issue of living more simply: how to live lives that are sustainable, just, and joyful.

REBECCA'S STORY

Changing lifestyle habits to be more sustainable can be difficult. Sometimes, an unexpected experience, like travel, propels us into a new lifestyle temporarily that may lead to permanent change. When Rebecca traveled and studied flamenco dance in Spain, she chose a one-bedroom apartment that was within her budget and close to transportation, activities, and dance classes. It had all the basics. The furniture was simple, but adequate. There was no television, radio or central heating. In the winter months, the temperature in Seville was 40 degrees Fahrenheit at night, so a small space heater was used to keep warm.

At first, Rebecca was apprehensive. How could she cook in such a small kitchen without a microwave and other electrical appliances? What would she do in the evenings without TV? Living in these new circumstances was a challenge and Rebecca soon discovered it was possible to cook a really good meal without a lot of electric appliances. She learned to dress in layers to keep warm and led an active social life. "A majority of the culture shares similar and simple ways of living. There is a lack of emphasis on consumer goods." It was a very happy time for Rebecca, in spite of the unaccustomed lifestyle.

Upon returning home to the United State, Rebecca began to evaluate her lifestyle and as a result, made changes to some of her ways of living. Most importantly, she realized that she could be happy without the many comforts and conveniences of American culture. When the economy took a nosedive and her investments took a hit, she was less stressed knowing she could live more simply and save money.

MARK'S STORY

When Mark traveled to Australia on a sabbatical, he volunteered for a couple who lived a consciously sustainable lifestyle with an organic food-growing practice called *permaculture*. The couple was mindful about their use of resources, especially water, paper and energy. They practiced composting, maintained a few chickens and sheep, and used native vegetation to minimize irrigation, fertilizer and pesticide use.

Exposure to these practices gave Mark a huge appreciation for sustainable choices, which he incorporated into his own life. While his condominium community did not permit growing organic food or maintaining animals, he minimized wasteful use of water, energy and paper. Mark also modified his driving choices to conserve gasoline. His family used heat and air conditioning sparingly and reduced unnecessary lighting. After a short while, these practices became automatic. They led to lower energy costs, and positively impacted the environment. Mark also shared what he had learned about the benefits of native vegetation with local gardens and merchants in his community.

Is there anything that holds you back from exploring simplicity in your life? What are your fears, doubts, and other barriers? Answer the following questions to better understand your point of view.

1. What concerns or barriers are keeping you from simplifying your life? _____

_____

_____

_____

_____

2. What are the upsides of simplicity? _____

_____

_____

_____

_____

_____

CREATE YOUR OWN CRYSTAL BALL

As you might suspect, the long-term approach to a sustainable lifestyle involves ongoing research and smart, proactive, in-depth planning. In Chapter 5, you explored the importance of intense research to uncover a career that is sustainable. Researching and staying aware of diminishing natural resources and economic changes in the world is equally important to your overall prosperity. The long-term approach requires that you keep one eye on the current conditions and another on the horizon.

Think back to the catastrophe of Hurricane Katrina. If you live in a coastal area that is vulnerable to changing weather conditions, planning ahead is vital to your survival. Evacuation is always a possibility, so it is prudent to keep important documents, phone numbers and business papers in one organized location that can be packed up in minutes. You also need to prepare storm kits with batteries, water, non-perishable foods and medications, in the event that power is out for several days. Being prepared for these situations allows you to adapt to emergency situations quickly.

Another example of being prepared involves the career front. Many states are dependent upon manufacturing jobs, and those types of jobs are often the first to go in economically depressed times. Moving to more employment-rich areas may be a necessity. This is not to dissuade you from working or living in these geographic areas, but if you do stay there, then you must be prepared for the not-known. Have an emergency plan in place.

Affordable lifestyle exercise

If you are currently in transition and your income or savings are lowered, this exercise can be an opportunity to make a correction. If you are presently in a good financial situation, it is still important, because your employment or savings could change in the future. Remember, the new norm is the not-known.

Worksheet:

In Chapter 6, you completed a financial worksheet. Go back to that exercise and use it as a reference to make adjustments or future corrections in lifestyle choices. Use the income and outflow numbers you entered on the sheet as a guideline for categories that need attention. Think both short- and long-term.

1. What is your upside to simplifying now? For example, what aspect of your lifestyle is unaffordable or too high: transportation, home mortgage, energy costs, eating out or vacations? _____

    _____

    _____

    _____

2. What activities can you adjust, recreate or eliminate? For example, if you love travel how can you travel more economically through home exchanges and volunteering?

    _____

    _____

    _____

    _____

3. In the long term, what economic and natural resource changes do you foresee that will affect you? For example, soaring gasoline prices, prolonged water shortages or severe weather patterns? _____

_____

_____

_____

_____

4. How will the above changes affect your lifestyle choices? For example, if your finances take another hit, will you have to rent, versus buying a house? If driving isn't affordable, will you move to a different location that provides better public transportation? If there are prolonged water shortages in your area, what personal choices will you make to scale back water usage? _____

_____

_____

_____

_____

5. What actions do you need to consider to prepare for the anticipated changes? _____

_____

_____

_____

_____

To help you through the process, the table on the next page offers categories of lifestyle alternatives.

Category	New Choices	Considerations
Housing	Reduce living space	Buy or rent? Roommates? Renting rooms?
Transportation	Hybrid car	Costs up front, biking, walking options
Energy use	Lower thermostat	Household items requiring less energy
Food	Buy local	Availability, time to prepare foods
Greening	Recycle, repurpose, reduce	Native plants vs. grass, filter water at home
Water use	Shorter showers, turn off water when shaving or brushing teeth	Retraining old habits, dish bin in the sink, hand-wash clothes, water-saving nozzles
Misc. expenses	Need vs. want	Entertain at home weekly, buy secondhand, resell unused items

SHORT- AND LONG-TERM LIFESTYLE ADJUSTMENTS

CASE STUDY

Paul and Jeanne bought a house they thought they could afford with two paychecks and subsequently took out a second mortgage to pay for a variety of expenses. They have one son in private school. Heating oil was expensive, and Jeanne drove to work. When Paul was laid off, they had to rearrange their lifestyle priorities to fit a reduced income. This is what they did:

1-3 MONTHS

- Review budget to determine what items can be reduced or eliminated.

- Investigate possible mortgage loan and credit card debt modifications.

- Reevaluate private versus public school options.

- Lower heat thermostat to save on heating oil; investigate small electric and wood-burning heaters instead of central heating.

- Shop in discount food stores; reduce meat and alcohol consumption; and plan meals for cost efficiency.

- Jeanne uses public transportation to save on gasoline.

- Potluck dinners with friends, instead of dining out; include kids to save on babysitting fees.

- Limit impulse buying to a fixed amount per week.

- Paul assumes child care and transportation duties instead of daycare center.

- Paul enrolls in state-sponsored programs for additional training.

4-9 MONTHS

- If Paul is still unemployed, investigate options of selling house and renting.

- Investigate day camp options versus summer boarding camp.

- Review budget again to see what can be further eliminated or adjusted.

- Research long-term sustainability of Paul's industry or profession.

- If unable to find work in his career field, Paul obtains career counseling and investigates new work options, including starting a small business.

- Research additional education or certification possibilities.

1-2 YEARS

- Paul completes additional schooling/training.

- Family considers relocating to a city or area with additional work opportunities, or where commuting expenses and time are less for the family.

SUMMARY

INTEGRATING YOUR PLAN INTO DAILY LIFE

There are many ways to change or flex your choices to fit the new norm. Like any major life change, this paradigm shift requires a change in your habits. Give yourself at least three to four months to start feeling comfortable with the new approaches you design.

To stay on track, follow these tips:

1. Develop a support group.

2. Reward yourself for small improvements.

3. Think all options through before choosing.

4. Keep a journal of changes and upsides.

5. Set goals that are manageable.

6. Stay focused. Remove distractions.

Reminders

- Review previous chapters and exercises.

- Analyze current lifestyle choices.

- Adapt short-term sustainability options.

- Anticipate and plan for long-term changes in economy, natural resources and climate change.

- Explore simplicity.

- Be aware of time management and your choices.

- Integrate choices with your personal career, core value, financial and success model.

CHAPTER 9

SUCCESS IS NOT SOLITARY: THE POWER OF PARTNERSHIPS

When we seek for connection, we restore the world to wholeness. Our seemingly separate lives become meaningful as we discover how truly necessary we are to each other.

~ Margaret Wheatley

It's been said that no man is an island; while solitude is important for reflection and planning, to enjoy sustainable success you need other people.

TIP #28

DEVELOP A COMMUNITY OF SUPPORT

During turbulent economic times, mutually beneficial partnerships are important. You'll need people who you believe and trust to encourage you and provide solid, caring advice. The upside of developing these strategic alliances is that they can help boost creativity and morale. Brainstorming with a carefully selected group of friends and/or colleagues is a vibrant tool to generate solutions and options outside your normal range of thinking.

Author, speaker and strategic alliance guru Ed Rigsbee has been promoting the power of alliances for more than 20 years. Rigsbee believes that developing mutually beneficial partnerships, or alliances, are more important than ever. "Business is more complex than ever before and a soft economy amplifies this complexity. As you continually seek solutions to your business challenges, why not access the synergy of additional views. Partnering with other business leaders to create a mastermind alliance is an answer to the idea of working smarter."

Start your own Dream Team

A Dream Team, or mastermind alliance, is a group of individuals who meet regularly to help each other brainstorm and problem-solve. Most teams operate best with four members. You don't need to know the members personally to invite them to be on your team. They can be experts in your field or people you admire. For optimum participation, however, there should be mutual reciprocation among all members, so consider what your group has to offer when inviting new members to join. It is not recommended to include family members, because they may find it difficult to be unbiased or objective.

Confidentiality is another key component. Your group may decide to sign a generic nondisclosure form. Some teams exclude more than one person from the same industry to avoid competition issues; others find that niche groups made up of

SUCCESS IS NOT
SOLITARY: THE POWER OF
PARTNERSHIPS

164

members from the same industry accelerate the brainstorming process. The key component to a working Dream Team is trust, so you may want to discuss the ways in which you will trust each other at your first meeting.

This Dream Team model is designed to meet monthly, but you can adjust your schedule based on the group's interests and needs. For a monthly meeting, consider following this agenda:

1. Schedule your meetings for one hour, with 15 minutes allotted to each member.

2. Each member presents a challenge, interest or need to the group. The group then brainstorms ideas and possible resources for the team member until the 15-minute allotment is up.

3. Another member takes notes for the presenter. This allows the member with the challenge to focus on the brainstorming instead of trying to record all ideas.

4. The only rule is that when your turn comes, you are not allowed to criticize or discount the team's suggestions with comments like, "That won't work, I don't have the money," or "I've tried that before." Instead, ask for clarification on how to make a suggestion work or for ideas to find funding.

5. At the end of the meeting, each person selects a goal or action plan to complete prior to the next meeting. You may want to set a deadline to report outcomes via e-mail before your meeting for greater efficiency.

6. If a member does not take action or make some effort toward their goal or ideal for two consecutive meetings, invite them to step down from the team until their

schedule permits them to focus on their results. This prevents less committed members from slowing down the group.

Most Dream Teams reach their optimum efficacy in about six to nine months, although some teams last longer by meeting less frequently. Your team's longevity depends on the outcomes you all want to reach; there is no right or wrong way to proceed, and you should intuitively be able to gauge when it is time to invite new members or disband the group.

USING ADVOCATES TO BUILD YOUR BUSINESS

To sustain and build your career, it is critical that you market your talents and availability to key decision-makers in your community or industry. Mark LeBlanc, author of *Growing Your Business*, recommends that you regularly contact the 25 most important people you know who are in a position to impact your business or career. He refers to these people as your advocates. Once a month, contact them by telephone or e-mail. Let them know what is new with your business, or send them a piece of information you think they might appreciate. Every few months, schedule a face-to-face meeting. Make sure that your relationship is mutually beneficial; the idea is to keep your business or services fresh in their mind, while also offering something of use to them. Expect to spend up to eight hours and $100 per month for this; if you are investing more than that, then you are making the process too complicated.

Cristine Thorn Ferguson, franchise owner of Cartridge World Greystone in Birmingham, Alabama uses Facebook to build strategic alliances. She created a Facebook fan page for her business that highlights a different client each week, with details about their business and contact information. She also reports how much money that client saved by buying their ink and toner cartridges directly from her. By promoting her clients' businesses as well as her own, she has developed a fiercely loyal client base.

As your relationship with one of these alliances develops, and you begin to conduct business transactions, you should consider formalizing the relationship with a contract. A contract is a smart idea, to protect the parties and clarify everyone's respective goals and expectations.

WHAT ABOUT THE NAY-SAYERS?

Creating sustainable success is still a cutting-edge idea and you are certain to encounter people who do not support your ideas or efforts, especially family members. It can be a tricky situation, because your natural inclination is to want the approval and assistance of those you respect and care about.

Put yourself in the other person's shoes before you share your ideas and dreams. Will your new plan or model create significant change for the other person? For example, George decided to leave his high-paying job as an executive to go back to school to study nursing. His wife, who was a stay-at-home mom, would now have to give up caring for her children and go back to work full-time to support her husband through school. Because this was not a personal goal for her, her initial reaction was understandably, not enthusiastic.

This does not mean that your family and friends do not care about you or love you—on the contrary. The people closest to you are also the most concerned for your well being. They are apt to play the devil's advocate, out of concern that you will be hurt or disappointed. Connie decided to start her own business after being laid-off and downsized twice in her field. Her husband responded by questioning her day-to-day business acumen, which hurt her feelings. Several years later, when she became very successful, her husband was motivated to start his own business. Nothing inspires support and enthusiasm like success, which is exactly why you need to cultivate outside resources to rekindle your energy and focus.

WORK YOUR NETWORK

In an era of online social networking, meeting face-to-face is still the best way to connect with future employers or individuals who can help you. Nothing beats a personal connection. A potential employer may receive thousands of online applications for a job; you can stand out by meeting him in person at a trade show or professional organization. And, even if you currently have a job, be sure to continue networking. Should your job or personal life situation change, you will have a good list of people to contact for help.

> *You need to see the whites of their eyes in order to truly evaluate a person. You can take charge of your career and personal life through relationships because they are built on trust.*
>
> ~ Lillian Bjorseth, professional networking expert and author

YOUR COMMUNITY AS A RESOURCE

Your community will likely offer a variety of programs, services and networks that can assist you with job opportunities, living situations, financial assistance and spiritual support. Whether it is a job or lifestyle change that you are seeking, use these resources for leads, fresh approaches and ongoing needs. Attending chamber of commerce meetings, entrepreneur/start up business groups and business networks can also help you find new opportunities in your work and personal life. Online resources abound.

Greg's story

When starting his freelance writing business, Greg became part of an informal small business support group, made up of individuals starting their own public relations, corporate consulting and screenwriting businesses. Greg used the group meetings as a sounding board for his ideas and plans. The group offered moral support and encouragement. Because the group was diverse, they had experience and connections in other areas of expertise and were able to provide resources for business plans, banking and health care. Eventually, group members forged friendships which lasted long after they had each achieved success.

Volunteering as a vehicle for new opportunities

Volunteering isn't just something to do while you have time on your hands. It is an excellent way to learn new skills, network and feel useful, all while helping others. If you have been out of work for a long time, your morale may be low. Having a place to go every day with other people, while focusing on a task that adds value to an organization, can be uplifting as well as productive. These meaningful activities also provide mental stimulation, which may help you come up with some creative solutions for your own work life. Whether you are interested in health care, the environment, child/elder care, pets or nonprofit organizations, volunteering for part of your week provides structure, learning, networking and maybe even a job, in the long-term.

To maximize your volunteering experience, follow these tips:

1. Volunteer in industries and areas that are related to the position you're trying to obtain.

2. Volunteer where you can utilize your current skills and/or develop new ones.

3. A long-term volunteer position will look good on your resume. On the other hand, short-term positions allow more diversity of experiences.

4. List your volunteer experience on your resume and discuss it in an interview.

5. Network with individuals at the volunteer job.

6. Identify and develop a relationship with members of a volunteer organization who may use your services in the future.

ASK AND YE SHALL RECEIVE

Don't forget to ask for help. When you are in crisis or transition, your self-esteem may suffer. It may be hard to admit and difficult to do, but reaching out during critical times actually accelerates your results. Whether it is a shoulder to cry on or someone with whom you can brainstorm, don't be shy about asking for support. Most people can relate to times in their own lives when they experienced losses and are willing to help you.

Reaching out for support can be a compliment for the other person. It relays trust and admiration for their skills and abilities. The act of asking, however, places you in a position of receiving, which can be difficult for the ego. It can make you feel vulnerable, but don't mistake that for weakness. By being open to receiving, you allow others to be generous and give of themselves, which can be a powerful bonding and relationship-building tool.

REMINDERS:

- Develop strategic partnerships.

- Coordinate or join a Dream Team.

- Communicate well with partners, family and friends.

- Stay in touch monthly with your Advocates list.

- Investigate community resources.

- Explore volunteering opportunities.

- Ask for help.

- Work your network.

CHAPTER 10

FROM CHAOS TO CLARITY

I've learned that making a "living" is not the same thing as making a "life."

~ Maya Angelou

Congratulations! The end is in sight—you're almost out of the rabbit hole. To achieve total clarity, the final step is to join the individual pieces of your plan into a whole-life design, forming a circle of sustainable success.

The circle of sustainable success is comprised of many categories. Each one is unique yet they are all connected in some way. The choices you make in each category will have a ripple effect on the others. Lifestyle choices affect your relationship to money and natural resources. Your inner core supports your choices and assists with your transitions. Simplicity—or lack thereof—affects your lifestyle, which spills over to your overall sustainability. Community and support systems provide the backbone of your career transition. As you continue to reflect on your life and work, keep in mind that this is a holistic process, and that it is always in flux as the not-known becomes known.

Circle of Sustainable Success

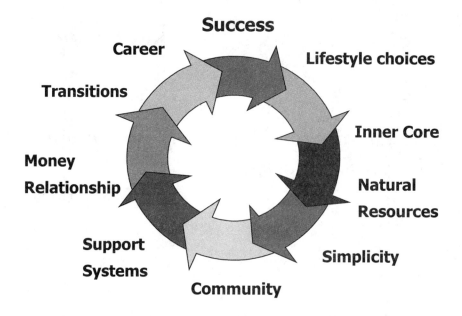

Remember these principles as you create your own circle of sustainable success:

- Be purposeful

- Keep an open mind

- Flow with surprises and change

- Be grateful for what you already have

JOIN THE CIRCLE OF SUSTAINABLE SUCCESS

Look over your answers to the exercises in each of the previous chapters. As you review the discoveries made in each chapter, notice how every item becomes an integral part of the completed circle. As a refresher, listed below are the tips for finding the upside and creating sustainable success.

CHAPTER 1   WAKE UP TO A NEW REALITY

#1 THE NOT-KNOWN IS THE NEW NORM

#2 CLARIFY YOUR CORE VALUES

#3 ABANDON THE MYTH OF JOB SECURITY

CHAPTER 2   GET OUT OF THE RABBIT HOLE

#4 LOOK BACK TO PLAN AHEAD

#5 BUST YOUR COMFORT ZONE BARRIERS

#6 MAKE LOSS AND CHANGE A SPRINGBOARD FOR SUCCESS

#7 ELIMINATE EXPECTATION AND ENTITLEMENT

#8 ATTITUDE = OUTCOMES

#9 PRACTICE RESILIENCE

Your journey is not a smooth or seamless experience. It is natural to get stuck or have difficulty with some of the exercises. Others have been where you are now and transitioned successfully. Consider the following stories of people who are happily living in the upside.

LEA'S STORY—APPLYING SUSTAINABLE PRINCIPLES

Lea adopted many of the principles presented in this book. She followed her passion, reevaluated her happiness and success models, took time out and adjusted her financial expectations and lifestyle. She was pleased with her success model.

Thirty-five years old and single, Lea had been employed in software marketing for four years when she was laid off. After searching for a year, she found a job in a nonprofit organization, which paid less than her former job.

The job-hunting process had its ups and downs. Initially, she looked for work in a frenzied way. She later moderated the time spent searching to allow for physical activities, like biking. She also took on miscellaneous jobs, such as cooking for others and volunteering. These activities gave her a sense of accomplishment and self-worth.

Lea had an opportunity to travel abroad with her mother to see her brother, who was working in India. At first she felt guilty, but in retrospect, it was like a mini-retirement. The time with her mother and brother was meaningful; it also gave her an opportunity to step back and analyze what she really wanted to do in her career—to determine what was important.

Because the new job paid less, Lea learned to manage her expenses. She readjusted her habits and saved up for important outings with friends. Because she worked at home, she saved on her wardrobe, gasoline and travel. When asked how she felt about making less money, she said, "I'm not money motivated. Job satisfaction is higher on the list."

Many of Lea's friends are still making more money than she is. This poses a challenge because she cannot afford the same social outings. In fact, she has very little discretionary money for entertainment. Lea may need to make new friends who have similarly modified their lifestyles to accommodate lower incomes.

JOYCE'S STORY—FINDING SUCCESS LATER IN LIFE

Joyce found her passion late in life. As a trained actress, producer and writer, she became dissatisfied with the opportunities the stage, TV and film industry offered; she had always liked politics. After researching the way politicians trained for on-camera and platform speeches, she discovered that many of them had no preparation or could not communicate their messages effectively. She started a niche business with a partner, offering consulting services to politicians—coaching, speech writing, editing and providing practice video sessions. As she gained more experience and made a name for herself, a Washington, D.C. training firm offered her a full-time position.

She loves her work, which offers a stimulating environment and endless opportunities to use her skills. She is happy to be working for a meaningful cause: electing good officials. The trade-off is separation from her partner and son who live in California. Hers is a commuting relationship, and her spouse supports her passion 100 percent.

JOANNE'S STORY—FINDING WORK/FAMILY BALANCE

Joanne was a successful lawyer and the principal breadwinner in her household. For 10 years she balanced work with the responsibilities of two children, while her husband completed a medical residency. But Joanne grew tired of the daily stress and a work environment that was not suited to her personality and values, so she left her well-paying position.

She and her husband adjusted their budget and lifestyle choices. Soon thereafter, her husband started a job, which alleviated some of the financial pressure. After adjusting to the fact that she didn't have a job, Joanne began to experience a newfound freedom. Her time off helped her to recover, mentally and physically, after years of stress and hard work. More time with her children was very rewarding. Following her passion for good food, Joanne took cooking lessons, which allowed her to use her creativity. She was much happier and surprised herself by concluding, "I never really liked my job."

After a while, Joanne began to think about the next steps in her career. Within two years, she was recruited for a job as a mediator in a university setting. The job offered her flexible hours and a workable salary, using the skills she had cultivated as a lawyer.

BOB'S STORY—HARNESSING SKILLS TO CREATE A NICHE

Bob's advertising career spanned 25 years at agencies in New York, Philadelphia and New Jersey. After losing a series of jobs as a result of economic conditions, he decided to start his own business as a freelance copywriter. Bob took an honest inventory of his skills and passions, and accurately identified an industry that would eagerly pay him for his talents.

He saw that there were many good copywriters who were terrified of any kind of technology, and many technology people who were terrible writers. His college degrees in both science and English allowed him to translate technical information into clear, compelling language that a businessperson with no technical training could read and understand. Identifying his power core traits placed Bob in a specialty niche market, with strong earning potential. His freelance business was a success.

BILL'S STORY—PARLAYING SKILLS AND EXPERIENCE INTO A BUSINESS

Bill was a producer for a home renovation show on public television. His show was purchased by a corporation that pushed it to new heights, but also created layoffs and reduced Bill's compensation considerably. Bill decided to leave the television industry and start his own consulting business. He negotiated a good severance pay to help him through the transition.

During his 17 years with the show, Bill earned a lot about home renovations. His no-nonsense approach appealed to clients, and eventually he built a strong consulting business offering insight and advice for assembling and managing the correct design and construction team.

LUCY'S STORY—VOLUNTEERING AND NETWORKING LEAD TO JOB

Lucy had always dreamed about being a community relations specialist. Her dead-end sales job was far from ideal. Then, she was laid off.

Lucy was already on the board of a charitable organization and decided to invest her newfound time to become more active. She also volunteered with other groups and went to every networking event available. At one point, Lucy was appointed to lobby her local state congress for one of the charities. The experience highlighted her persuasive communication skills and allowed her to make influential networking contacts.

Lucy eventually interviewed for a marketing position in the recovery field. Based on her philanthropic experience, passion, energy and considerable skills from the various volunteer positions, her new employer not only gave her the job, but changed the title for her to Community Relations Specialist.

BECKY'S STORY—FOLLOWING INTUITION THROUGH SEVERAL CAREERS

When it comes to Becky's career choices and personal life, she has followed her intuition to a wide variety of experiences. Years ago, she quit her corporate job and moved to a new city to study to become a massage therapist and Reiki master. Before then, she waited tables, wrote screenplays, learned about astrology and directed murder mysteries. Later in life, her spirit led her to attend law school and move yet again, this time to Washington, D.C., in pursuit of a human trafficking fellowship, while volunteering for Amnesty International.

Regardless of the experience, Becky is always content where she is and never considers any of it wasted time. She has no regrets. She trusts that every experience will provide a lesson or contact for use down the road and is open to the possibility that a new path will reveal itself. She knows that she cannot see the future, and has chosen to trust that her life will unfold exactly as it is supposed to.

SOUNDS GOOD, BUT ...

You can count on a few obstacles in your transition. When this happens, revisit the exercise or chapter that identifies the barrier and consider investigating the resources provided at the end of the book. A quick review of the chapters is listed below for easy reference.

Chapter 1

1. How is the new norm affecting your sustainable success model? _____

   _____

   _____

   _____

Chapter 2

2. Have your core values changed or been clarified? Explain.

   _____

   _____

   _____

   _____

3. Any new revelations regarding past choices and lessons learned? What must you change to succeed? _____

   _____

   _____

   _____

   _____

4. Which decisions contributed to your success and happiness?_____

   _____

   _____

   _____

Chapter 3

5. What have you learned about yourself in relationship to entitlements? Do they exist? Do they contribute to your well-being or act as barriers? _____

_____

_____

6. Do you feel that using resiliency practices in your everyday life is helping? _____

_____

_____

7. Who are your mentors now? _____

_____

_____

8. Are you aware of any changes in your attitude that are having positive affects on your life?_____

_____

_____

9. How do gratefulness practices affect your daily life? _____

_____

_____

10. Comment on current expectations and attachments. _____

_____

_____

11. What are you doing for fun? _____

_____

_____

12. Have you taken the time to experience and explore the stages of transition? _____

_____

Chapter 4

13. What factors are missing in you life now that could add to your success and happiness definition? _____

   _____

   _____

14. Finish the following sentences:

   I get really excited about my life when _____

   _____

   _____

   _____

   I am happiest when _____

   _____

   _____

   _____

15. What new influences have you brought to your success model? _____

   _____

   _____

Chapter 5

16. What new career possibilities have you explored beyond your comfort level? _____

   _____

   _____

17. Who in your circle of family, friends and colleagues have you asked for feedback and ideas?_____

   _____

   _____

18. Have you set time aside to be still with your thoughts? ____

_____

_____

19. What are you reading, researching or learning to assist with your career plan?_____

_____

_____

20. Do you take time to daydream? _____

_____

_____

21. What thoughts and ideas in your journal have been helpful?

_____

_____

_____

22. Have you developed a support group—people and places that inspire hope? _____

_____

_____

23. How are you using the perceived chaos in your life to experiment and explore? _____

_____

_____

24. Have you tried new activities to spark creativity, such as a hobby, travel or volunteering? _____

_____

_____

25. What new trends have you uncovered to help you with your career? _____

_____

26. How are you using the power core activity? _____

_____

_____

27. What new marketable skills have you uncovered? _____

_____

_____

28. Has your passion changed? _____

_____

_____

Chapter 6

29. Where are you now in your financial plan? Identify the changes. _____

_____

_____

30. Have you made any changes in the need versus want perspective? _____

_____

_____

31. Are you able to live within your means? _____

_____

_____

32. Are there any changes in your prosperity definition? _____

_____

_____

33. Have you disposed of any credit cards? Are you using them more or less? _____

_____

_____

34. Describe new ways you are being resourceful to get what you need without a lot of debt._____

_____

_____

35. Are you using a financial planner to keep your income and outflow balanced? _____

_____

_____

Chapter 7

36. Personal mission statements—have they changed? _____

_____

_____

_____

37. The most satisfying professional experiences in my life are:

_____

_____

_____

38. The most satisfying personal experiences in my life are: __

_____

_____

_____

39. What mindfulness activities are you using to help you stay focused? _____

_____

_____

Chapter 8

40. How do your current lifestyle choices coordinate with your budget? _____

   _____

   _____

41. Have you implemented simplicity in your daily life? Has it changed your perception of success and happiness? _____

   _____

   _____

   _____

Chapter 9

42. Describe how you are using the following support systems to help you.

   • Mastermind groups _____

      _____

      _____

   • Networks _____

      _____

      _____

   • Community resources_____

      _____

      _____

43. Have you volunteered to help you achieve your goals? ____

   _____

   _____

44. Do you ask for help? _____

   _____

Chapter 10

45. List your goals for the next six months to one year. _____

_____

_____

_____

_____

_____

46. List your goals for the next one to two years. _____

_____

_____

_____

_____

_____

47. List your goals for the next two to three years._____

_____

_____

_____

_____

_____

48. List your goals for the next three to four years. _____

_____

_____

_____

_____

_____

49. List your goals for the next five years. _____

_____

_____

_____

_____

We wish you a successful journey to the upside as you create your own sustainable success. Keep in mind the words of Ralph Waldo Emerson:

Success: To laugh often and much, to win the respect of intelligent people and the affection of children, to earn the appreciation of honest critics and endure the betrayal of false friends, to appreciate beauty, to find the best in others, to leave the world a bit better, whether by a healthy child, a garden patch, or a redeemed social condition; to know even one life has breathed easier because you have lived. This is to have succeeded!

BIBLIOGRAPHY AND RESOURCES

Chapter 1

Assadourian, Erik. "The Rise and Fall of Consumer Cultures."
In *The State of the World 2010, From Consumerism to
Sustainability*. Washington, D.C.: Worldwatch Institute, 2010.

Blankenship, Allison. Organic Success.
www.myorganicsuccess.com.

Brooks, David. "The Culture of Debt." *New York Times,*
July 22, 2008.

Carkhuff, Robert R. Saving America! The Generativity
Solution. www.generativitysolution.com.

Cox, Amanda, Kevi Quealy, and Amy Schoenfeld. "For the
Unemployed, a Day Stacks Up Differently." *New York Times,*
August 2, 2009, Soapbox.

Duany, Andres and Plater-Zyberk, and Elizabeth and Jeff Speck.
*Suburban Nation: The Rise of Sprawl and the Decline of the
American Dream.* New York: North Point Press, 2001.

Federal Deposit Insurance Corporation. www.fdic.gov
(Sheila Blair, chairwoman).

Fox, Matthew. *The Reinvention of Work: A New Vision of
Livelihood for Our Time.* San Francisco: Harper, 1995.

Friedman, Thomas. *Hot, Flat and Crowded: Why We Need a
Green Revolution.* New York: Farrar, Straus, Giroux, 2008.

Gates, Bill. www.microsoft.com/presspass/exec/billg/.

Goodman, Peter S. "On Every Front Anxious Questions and
Discomfiting Answers." *New York Times,* July 19, 2008.

Hampsen, Rick. "A World Forever Changed: Decade Defined
by Technology, Terror, Recession, Elections." *USA Today,*
December 22, 2009.

Healthfield, Susan M, About.com guide to human resources. www.about.com.

Jarvis, Gail Marks. "A Worrisome Picture." *Chicago Tribune*, July 23, 2009.

Korkki, Phylis. "Accentuating the Positive After a Layoff." *New York Times*, August 16, 2009.

Kristoff, Nicholas D. "The Downturn's Upside." *New York Times*, October 19, 2008.

Krugman, Paul. "That 1937 Feeling." *New York Times*, January 4, 2009

Langley, Noel, Florence Ryerson, and Edgar Allan Woolf. *The Wizard of Oz.* Directed by Victor Fleming. Hollywood, California: Metro-Goldwyn-Mayer, 1939.

Lee, Don. "Bernanke: U.S. Is in for a Very Long Haul." *Tribunes Newspapers*, July 23, 2009.

McIntyre, Douglas. "The Recession America Needed." *Newsweek*, August 4, 2009. www.newsweek.com/id/210390.

McKibben, Bill. *Deep Economy: The Wealth of Communities and the Durable Future.* New York: Henry Holt, 2007.

Mitchell, Pamela. Reinvention Institute. www.reinvention-institute.com.

Morgenson, Gretchen. "Given a Shovel, Digging Deeper Into Debt." *New York Times*, July 20, 2008.

Peck, Dennis. "Does Our Health Actually Get Better in Some Ways During a Down Economy?" OregonLive.com (April 22, 2009). www.oregonlive.com/health/index. ssf/2009/04/does_our_health_actually_get_b.html.

Popcorn, Faith. Brain Reserve. www.faithpopcorn.com.

Pulley, Mary Lynn. *Losing Your Job—Reclaiming Your Soul.* San Francisco: Jossey-Bass Inc., 1997.

Reich, Robert. www.robertreich.org.

Ruhm, CJ. "Healthy Living in Hard Times." *Journal of Health Economics* (2005): 341-363.

Schor, Juliet B. *The Overworked American: The Unexpected Decline of Leisure.* New York: BasicBooks, 1993. www2.bc.edu/~schorj/.

Shi, David. "Get Lost en Route to Getting Found." *Atlanta Journal-Constitution*, July 24, 2009.

Shiller, Robert J. "Stuck in Neutral? Reset the Mood." *New York Times*, January 31, 2010.

Silverstein, Sam. *The Success Model: The Five-Step System to Completely Revolutionize Your Life!* Virginia: Star Publishing, 1993.

Stiglitz, Joseph E. America, *Free Markets and the Sinking of the World Economy.* New York: WW Norton & Company, 2010.

Uchilette, Louis. "Women Are Now Equal As Victims of Poor Economy." *New York Times*, July 22, 2008.

Chapter 2

Carroll, Lewis. *Alice in Wonderland.* UK: Macmillian, 1864.

Chodron, Pema. *Comfortable with Uncertainty.* Boston: Shambhala, 2002.

Cohen, Gail. *Thinking Outside the Lines,* Audio series. Kansas: National Press Publications, July 2000.

Dyer, Wayne. *Change Your Thoughts, Change Your Life.* California: Hay House, 2009. www.drwaynedyer.com.

Michaels, Bonnie and Michael Seef. *A Journey of Work-Life Renewal: the Power to Recharge and Rekindle Passion in Your Life.* Chicago: Managing Work & Family, Inc., 2003.

Myss, Carolyn. *Anatomy of the Spirit.* New York: Crown Publishers, 1997. www.myss.com.

Robinson, Anthony B. "Articles of Faith: The Unfortunate Age of Entitlement in America." *Seattle Post-Intelligencer*, March 23, 2007.

Sheerer, Robin. *No More Blue Mondays: Four Keys to Finding Fulfillment at Work*. California: Davies-Black, 1999. www.robinsheerer.com.

Stern, Seth. "The Boomers Raised an Entitlement Generation." *The Rocky Mountain Collegian*, 2009. http://www.collegian. com/index.php/article/2009/04/the_boomers_raised_ an_entitlement_generation.

Chapter 3

Bridges, William. *Transitions: Making Sense of Life's Changes*. Massachusetts: Da Capo Press, 2004.

Covey, Steven. www.stevencovey.com.

Finney, Martha. *Rebound: A Proven Plan for Starting Over After Job Loss*. New Jersey: Pearson Education, 2009.

Hall, Sylvia. *No Fear*. New York: Scholastic Press, 2001.

Johnston, Paul Dennisthorne. "Here and Now, Less Worry." *ETC.: A Review of General Semantics*, International Society for General Semantics Vol. 53, 1996.

Manton, Jim. *The Secret of Transitions: How to Move Effortlessly to Higher Levels of Success*. Oregon: Robert Reed Publishers, 2008.

Mathison, Duncan and Martha Finney. *Unlock the Hidden Job Market*. New Jersey: Pearson Education, 2010.

Molitor, Nancy, public education coordinator for American Psychological Association. www.APA.org.

Neal, Judi. *Edgewalkers: People and Organizations that Take Risks, Build Bridges and Break New Ground*. Connecticut: Praeger, 2006.

Pribyl, Lukas. *Forgotten Transports*, documentary, 2010.

Siewert, Joan. *No Fear in Love*, 1996.

Sorenstein, Seth. "To Scientists, Laughter is no Joke—It's Serious." *Naples Daily News*, April 1, 2010.

Varley, Patricia, featured author. *Power Tools: Top Executive Coaches Put You on the Fast Track to Success*. Compass Series Publishing, 2006. www.patriciavarley.com.

Varley, Patricia, featured author. *Successfully Navigating Through Change and Transition: Finding the Eye in the Hurricane*. www.patriciavarley.com.

Varley, Patricia. *Because you Matter: 10 Heart-Centered Principles for Living the Life You Desire*, workbook and teleclass. www.patriciavarley.com.

Wood, John T. What *Are You Afraid of? : A Guide to Dealing with Your Fears*. New Jersey: Prentice Hall (1976).

Chapter 4

Assadourian, Erik. "The Rise and Fall of Consumer Cultures." In *The State of the World 2010, From Consumerism to Sustainability*. Washington, D.C.: Worldwatch Institute, 2010.

Bhutan Center of Gross National Happiness. www.grossnationalhappiness.com

Canfield, Jack and Janet Switzer. *The Success Principles: How to Get from Where You Are to Where You Want To Be*. New York: HarperCollins, 2005.

Chopra, Deepak. *The Seven Spiritual Laws of Success*. California: New World Library, 1994.

Dolgoff, Stephanie. "Create Your Own Happy-Life List!" *Self Magazine*, Aug 21, 2008.

Gibbs, Nancy. "Happiness Paradox: Why Are Americans So Cheery?" *Time*, November 23, 2009.

Gilbert, Daniel. *Stumbling on Happiness*. New York: Alfred A. Knopf, 2006.

Harris, Russ. *The Happiness Trap: How to Stop Struggling and Start Living*. MA: Trumpeter, June 3, 2008.

Lyubormirsky, Sonja. *The How of Happiness: A Scientific Approach to Getting the Life You Want*. New York: Penguin Press, 2008.

Lyubomirsky, Sonja, David Schaade and Kennon Sheldon. "Pursuing Happiness: The Architecture of Sustainable Change." *Review of General Psychology* 9 (2005): 111-131.

Lyubomirsky, Sonja. "Why We're Still Happy." *New York Times,* December 26, 2008.

Mayer, Jeffrey. *Success is a Journey: 7 Steps to Achieving Success in the Business of Life*. New York: McGraw-Hill, 1999.

Myers, David G. and Ed Diener. "Who is Happy?" *Psychological Science* 6 (1995): 10-17.

Porraas, Jerry, Stewart Emery and Mark Thompson. *Success Built to Last: Creating a Life that Matters.* New York: Plume, 2007.

Pozzi, Doris and Dorian Welles. *Success with Soul: New Insights to Achieving Success with Real Meaning*. Seattle: Dorian Welles, 1997.

Ricard, Matthieu. *Happiness: A Guide to Developing Life's Most Important Skill*. MA: Little, Brown and Company, 2007.

Shimoff, Marci and Carol Kline. *Happy for No Reason: 7 Steps to Being Happy from the Inside Out*. New York: Free Press, 2008.

Williams Sr., Thaddeus M. *Positioning Yourself: How to Transition for Happiness, Peace, and Prosperity.* New York: Author House, 2009.

Chapter 5

"America's Best Careers 2010." *U.S. News & World Report*.
   http://www.usnews.com/sections/business/best-careers/.

American Society for Training and Development.
   www.astd.org.

Asher, Donald. *How to Get Any Job: Life Launch and Re-Launch
   For Everyone Under 30*. New York:
   Ten Speed, 2004 (2nd Edition).

Bailin, Jenny Hourihan. "Out of a Job, and Realizing Change Is
   Good." *New York Times*, October 26, 2008, Openers.

Blankenship, Allison. "Harness the Power of a Life Diva
   Mastermind Group to Achieve Your Goals." Life Divas.
   http://www.lifedivas.com/PDFs/Mastermind_Group.pdf.

Boldt, Laurence G. *How to Find the Work You Love*.
   New York: Arkana, 1996.

"Business Statistics." Byte Start. www.bytestart.co.uk/content/
   news/statistics/

Career Builder. www.careerbuilder.com/.

Career Overview. www.careeroverview.com.

"Career Resources Toolkit for Job-Seekers." Quintessential
   Careers. www.quintcareers.com/career_resources.html.

Career Websites. www.careerwebsites.com.

Careers.org. www.careers.org.

Clark, Tony. "Who's Defining Your Model of Success?" Success
   from the Nest. http://successfromthenest.com/content/
   whos-defining-your-model-of-success/.

"Dream Green Jobs." Sustainable Business.
   www.greendreamjobs.com

Eberstadt, Nick and Ken Gronbach. "The Age Curve Report."
   Age Curve Report. http://www.theagecurvereport.com/
   newsletter.html.

Glanz, Barbara. Barbara Glanz Communications.
    www.barbaraglanz.com.

Gumpel, Eve. "Cater to Women if you Want Success."
    Women Entrepreneur. http://www.womenentrepreneur.
    com/2009/08/cater-to-women-if-you-want-success.html.

Harkness, Helen. *Capitalizing on Career Chaos, Bringing
    Creativity and Purpose to Your Work and Life.*
    California: Davies-Black Publishing, 2005.

Kaye, Beverly. Up Is Not the Only Way: *A Guide to Developing
    Workforce Talent.* Boston: Intercultural Press, 2002.
    www.careersystemsintl.com

"Key Facts about Women-Owned Businesses." Center
    for Women's Business Research. http://www.
    womensbusinessresearchcenter.org/research/keyfacts/.

Lansky, Judith. President-Lansky Careers. twitter.com/
    lanskycareers. 312-494-0022.

Mackay, Harvey. *Use Your Head to Get Your Foot in the Door: Job
    Search Secrets No One Else Will Tell You.* UK: Portfolio, 2010.

Marling, Saundra and Jill Pfaff-Waterbury. *Boomers' Job Search
    Guide.* Life Transition Consulting, 2006.

Mathison, Duncan and Martha Finney. *Unlock the Hidden Job
    Market: 6 Steps to a Successful Job Search When Times are
    Tough.* New Jersey: FT Press, 2009.

McGaughey Jr., William. "Information and Writings Which
    Favor Government Action to Reduce Work Time."
    ShorterWorkWeek.com. www.shorterworkweek.com.

Money/Careers Section. *U.S. News & World Report.*
    www.usnews.com/sections/business/best-careers/.

Musolino, Michael. Make Good Choices! Apparel with a
    Positive Edge. www.imakegoodchoices.com.

National Career Development Association. *www.ncda.org.*

Nemko, Marty. "15 Hot Jobs in a (Gulp!) Depression." *U.S. News & World Report*. www.usnews.com/articles/business/careers/2009/10/27/15-hot-jobs-in-a-gulp-depression.html.

"One of the World's Leading Sources of New Business Ideas." Springwise. www.springwise.com.

Orman, Suze. www.suzeorman.com.

Peck, Don. "How a New Jobless Era Will Transform America." *The Atlantic*, March, 2010.

Pope, Elizabeth. "Matching Life Experience With New Careers." *New York Times*, March 3, 2010.

Ryan, Robert. *Over 40 & You're Hired! Secrets to Landing a Great Job*. New York: Penguin, 2010.

"Search Marketing Jobs." Marketing Ladder. www.mktgladder.com.

Shahnasarian, Michael. *Decision Time: A Guide to Career Enhancement*. Oklahoma: National Career Development Association, 2006.

"Small Biz Stats & Trends." SCORE. www.score.org/small_biz_stats.html.

SmartBlog on Workforce. smartblogs.com/workforce/.

Society for Human Resource Management. www.shrm.org.

Springwise. www.springwise.com.

"Top Industries to Work In." Inc.com. http://www.inc.com/multimedia/slideshows/content/top-industries-06_pagen_1.html.

Tulgan, Bruce. www.rainmakerthinking.com.

U.S. Small Business Administration. www.sba.gov.

Wagele, Elizabeth and Ingrid Stabb. *The Career Within You: How to Find the Perfect Job for Your Personality*. New York: HarperOne, 2010.

Whitefield, Edwin A., Rich Feller, and Chris Wood, ed.
    A Counselor's Guide to Career Assessment Instruments.
    Oklahoma: National Career Development Association, 2009.

Williams, Alex. "Say Hello to Underachieving." *New Times,*
    July 5, 2009, Sunday Styles section.

Winter, Barbara J. *Making a Living Without a Job: Winning*
    Ways for Creating Work that You Love. New York:
    Bantam Doubleday Dell, 1993.

"Work with a Startup." JobNob. www.jobnob.com.

World at Work. www.worldatwork.org.

Yahoo! Hotjobs search engine. http://hotjobs.yahoo.com/
    HotJobs100/index.html.

Chapter 6

Bach, David. *Start Over, Finish Rich: 10 Steps to Get You Back on*
    Track in 2009. New York: Broadway Books, 2009.

Burch, Mark A. *Simplicity: Notes, Stories and Exercises for*
    Developing Unimaginable Wealth. Gabriola Island, B.C.:
    New Society Publishers, 1995.

Cascio, Jamais. "Resilience." *Foreign Policy.* May/Jun 2009.

Chatzky, Jean. *You Don't Have to be Rich.* United Kingdom:
    Portfolio, Penguin Imprint, 2003.

Dappen, Andy. *Shattering the Two-Income Myth: Daily Secrets for*
    Living Well on One Income. Washington: Brier Books, 1997.

Dominguez, Joe. *Transforming Your Relationship with Money.*
    Colorado: Sounds True, 2005.

Eker, Harv. *Secrets of the Millionaire Mind.* New York:
    Harper Collins, 2005.

Fisher, Davis. Money Tree Consulting.
    www.moneytreeconsulting.com.

Gage, Randy. *101 Keys to Prosperity.* Kansas: Prime Concepts
    Group, Inc., 2003.

The Herman Report. www.hermanreport.com.

Howard, Clark. http://clarkhoward.com.

Internal Revenue Service. www.IRS.gov.

Mercer Consulting. www.mercer.com.

Sapadin, Linda. *Master Your Fears: How to Triumph over Your Worries and Get on with Your Life.* New Jersey: Wiley, 2004.

Shepherd, Margaret. *Cash and Consciousness: 21 Days to Abundance.* Wyoming: Crowheart Media, 2007.

Twist, Lynne. *The Soul of Money: Transforming Your Relationship with Money and Life.* New York: W. W. Norton & Company, 2003.

Uchitelle, Louis. "Spending Stalls, and Businesses Slash." *U.S. Jobs,* 2009.

Winget, Larry. *You're Broke Because You Want to Be.* New York: Gotham Books, 2008.

Chapter 7

Eker, Harv. *Secrets of the Millionaire Mind.* New York: Harper Collins, 2005.

Gergen, Kenneth, senior research professor, Swarthmore College. http://www.swarthmore.edu/x20604.xml.

Harkness, Helen. *Capitalizing on Career Chaos, Bringing Creativity and Purpose to Your Work and Life.* California: Davies-Black Publishing, 2005.

Kabat-Zinn, Jon. *Wherever You Go There You Are: Mindfulness Meditation in Everyday Life.* New York: Hyperion, 1994.

Levey, Joel and Michelle. Inner Work Technologies. www.wisdomatwork.com

Levey, Joel and Michelle. *Living in Balance.* California: Conari Press, 1998.

Levey, Joel and Michelle. *Luminous Mind: Meditation & Mind Fitness.* San Francisco: Red Wheel/Weiser, 2009.

McGaughey Jr., William. "Information and Writings Which Favor Government Action to Reduce Work Time." ShorterWorkWeek.com. www.shorterworkweek.com.

Moore, Thomas. *Care of the Soul: A Guide for Cultivating Depth and Sacredness in Everyday Life*. New York: Harper Perennial, 1994.

Rowe, Jonathan. "Wasted Work, Wasted Time." In *Take Back Your Time*. San Francisco: Berrett-Koehler Publishers, 2003.

Shambhala Magazine. www.shambhalasun.com.

Take Back Your Time. www.timeday.org.

Tolle, Echkart. *The Power of Now*. California: New World Library, 2004.

Varley, Patricia, executive life coach and author. www.patriciavarley.com.

Chapter 8

Andrews, Cecile and Wanda Urbanska. *Less Is More*. Canada: New Society, 2009.

Aslet, Don. *Clutter's Last Stand: It's Time to De-Junk Your Life!* Idaho: Marsh Creek Press, 2005.

Beavan, Colin. *No Impact Man*. New York: Farrar, Straus and Giroux, 2009.

Blix, Jacqueline and David Heitmiller. *Getting a Life: Strategies for Simple Living Based on the Revolutionary Program for Financial Freedom from Your Money or Your Life*. New York: Viking Penguin, 1999.

Blumenthal, Ralph and Rachel Mosteller. "Imagine No Possessions." *New York Times*, May 17, 2008.

Brown, Lester R. *Eco-Economy: Building an Economy for the Earth*. New York: W.W. Norton, 2001.

Cave, Damien, and Marjorie Connelly. "Americans Doing More, Buying Less." *New York Times*, January 3, 2010.

Darlin, Damon. "A Lesson in Frugality, From the Tenements."
New York Times, December 13, 2009.

de Graaf, John, Thomas Naylor and David Wann. *Affluenza:
The All-Consuming Epidemic.* San Francisco:
Berrett-Koehler, 2001.

de Graaf, John, ed. *Take Back Your Time: Fighting Overwork and
Time Poverty in America.* San Francisco:
Berrett-Koehler, 2003.

Dietzel, William H. *Common Sense Lifestyle for the 21st Century.*
Oklahoma: Tate Publishing, 2008.

Drake, John D. *Downshifting: How to Work Less and Enjoy Life
More.* San Francisco: Berrett-Koehler, 2001.

Elgin, Duane. *Voluntary Simplicity: Toward the Way of Life That
Is Outwardly Simple, Inwardly Rich.* New York: Quill, 1993.

Free exchange websites to trade goods and services with
others worldwide: Freecycle.org; Goozex.com (video
games); Neighborrow.com; PaperbackSwap.com (books);
SwapaDVD.com (DVDs); SwapStyle.com (fashion);
Zwaggle.com (baby & children's gear).

Friedman, Thomas L. "Connecting Nature's Dots."
New York Times, August 23, 2009.

Gould, Rebecca Kneale. *At Home in Nature.* California:
University of California Press, 2005.

Heath, Chip and Dan. *Make Changes that Last.* New York:
Broadway Books, 2010.

Heim, Joanne. *Living Simply: Choosing Less in a World of More.*
CO: Multnomah Books, 2006.

Hochschild, Arlie Russell. *The Time Bind: When Work Becomes
Home and Home Becomes Work.* New York: Owl Books, 2001.

Kasser, Tim. *High Price of Materialism.* Cambridge, MA:
MIT Press, 2002.

Koch, Wendy. "In Recession, a Simple 'Silver Lining.'"
   USA Today, July 13, 2009.

Kristof, Nicholas D. "What Could You Live Without?"
   New York Times, January 3, 2010.

Krugman, Paul. "Stranded in Suburbia." *New York Times*,
   May 13, 2008.

The Lazy Environmentalist. www.lazyenvironmentalist.com.

Lin, Derek. *The Tao of Daily Life*. New York: Jeremy P. Tarcher/
   Penguin, 2007.

Luhrs, Janet. *The Simple Living Guide*. New York:
   Broadway Books, 1997.

Lyall, Sarah. "Dear Prudence: Recession May Bring Return of
   Traditional Values." *New York Times*, October 21, 2008.

Marks, Tod. "Shop smart to save big at the supermarket."
   Consumerreports.org/Money, Spring, 2009.

Morgenstern, Julie. *SHED Your Stuff & Change Your Life: a Four-
   Step Guide to Getting Unstuck*. New York: Fireside, 2009.

O'Keefe, Cathy, instructor in therapeutic recreation and
   leisure studies, University of South Alabama.
   http://www.southalabama.edu/coe/hpels/faculty.shtml.

Onearth Magazine. Natural Resources Defense Council.
   www.onearth.org.

Robinson, Joe. *Work to Live: The Guide to Getting a Life*.
   New York: Perigee, 2003.

Rowe, Jonathan. "Wasted Work, Wasted Time." In *Take Back
   Your Time*. San Francisco: Berrett-Koehler
   Publishers, Inc., 2003.

Salwen, Kevin and Hannah. *The Power of Half*. Illinois:
   Houghten Mifflin Harcourt, 2010.

Segal, David. "Plan B." *New York Times*, February 8, 2009.

Schnumberger, Lynn. "Live Well With What You Have."
   Parade, January 10, 2010.

Shi, David E. "Americans May Come to Cherish their Forced Frugality." *Atlanta Journal Constitution*, March 27, 2009.

Shi, David E. *The Simple Life: Plain Living and High Thinking in American Culture.* Athens, Georgia: University of Georgia Press, 2001.

The Story of Stuff Project. www.storyofstuff.com.

Take Back Your Time. www.timeday.org.

Wann, David. *Simple Prosperity: Finding Real Wealth in a Sustainable Lifestyle.* New York: St. Martin's Griffin, 2007.

Yes! Magazine. www.yesmagazine.org.

Chapter 9

Bennett, Charles. "Volunteering: The Selfish Benefits: Achieve Deep-Down Satisfaction and Create That Desire in Others." Committee Communications, June 1, 2001.

Bjorseth, Lillian. *Breakthrough Networking: Building Relationships That Last.* Illinois: Duoforce Enterprises, Inc., 2009.

Cartridge World Greystone (Birmingham, AL franchise). www.cwgreystone.com (Cristine Ferguson, owner).

Community social services locator. www.communityresources.net.

Dream Team Mastermind Groups. www.LifeDivas.com.

LeBlanc, Mark. *Growing Your Business!* MN: Expert Publishing, Inc., 2003.

Rigsbee, Ed, strategic alliance consultant, author and speaker. www.Rigsbee.com

Rosenberg, Bob. *Giving from Your Heart: A Guide to Volunteering.* iUniverse, Inc., 2005.

Topic interest groups. www.meetup.com.

Chapter 10

Baker, Bob. www.technicalcopytogo.com.

Design New England. http://digital.designnewengland.com/designnewengland/20090708#pg1.

Help a Reporter Out. www.helpareporter.com.

ABOUT THE AUTHOR
BONNIE MICHAELS

Bonnie Michaels is president of Managing Work & Family, Inc, a work-life consulting and training firm since 1987, which is dedicated to helping organizations and workers solve work- and personal-life conflicts. Her many U.S. and international clients span across all industries. Since the downturn in the economy she has turned her attention to helping individuals through difficult career, financial and lifestyle transitions, while creating a life that is sustainable during changing times.

Bonnie combines first hand knowledge, practical ideas and inspiration in her presentations. As a trained actress, she brings outstanding speaking skills to her many platform speeches and training programs. She is a regular contributor to radio, TV and print stories. In addition, she co-authored, *Solving the Work/Family Puzzle* and *A Journey of Work-Life Renewal, the Power to Recharge & Rekindle the Passion in Life.*

Bonnie walks the talk to maintain her own balance. In 2000 she took a year-long renewal journey volunteering, studying Flamenco and experiencing alternative lifestyles. This life-changing journey greatly influenced her current and more sustainable lifestyle on which she writes and speaks.

As a local and national activist, she is on the executive board for Take Back Your Time and volunteers at the Conservancy of SW Florida, League of Women Voters, and environmental networks. Over the last two decades, she has been a member of the National Speakers Association, Association of Training and Development, Society for Human Resources, Women in Film/Chicago, SW Florida Brandeis Chapter and World at Work. She is on the Women's Bureau Working Women Honor Roll.

Bonnie has a B.A. in Early Childhood Education from Northeastern University, Montessori Certification, and has taken continuing education courses in business management, training, communication, psychology, and film. She is passionate about flamenco dancing and hiking. She is married with three children and seven grandchildren.

For more information, visit:
website: www.mwfam.com
email: mwfam@aol.com
or call 847-308-0919

ABOUT THE AUTHOR
ALLISON BLANKENSHIP

Allison Blankenship is the go-to person for accelerating results. With a career spanning two decades, she excels in developing and implementing new ideas, strategies and start-ups within organizations.

Allison uses her vast experience as a corporate entrepreneur and award-winning communication skills to empower people to perform under pressure. Having personally lost two jobs – one to a corporate bankruptcy and another to reorganization – she brings practical, real-life strategies and solutions to individuals and organizations.

Allison has developed two breakthrough systems to perform under pressure: Precision Speaking Systems, which creates confident communicators and presenters; and Organic Success, which transforms organizations by developing individual talents and abilities into competitive advantages that increase productivity.

She has co-authored three books, plus multiple audio series and training curriculums. Allison is the recipient of multiple awards including *Outstanding Young Woman of America, Speaker of the Year,* and *Jim Barber Leadership Award* for the state of Florida. She is the past president of the Florida Speaker's Association and a member of the National Speakers Association, American Society of Training and Development, American Business Women's Association and various philanthropic boards.

Allison graduated cum laude from Auburn University with a BA in Mass Communications and is one of the first 100 Accredited Public Relations Professionals in Florida. She shares her time between offices in Birmingham, AL and Naples, FL with her husband and two children.

For more information, visit:
the online press kit: www.AllisonSpeaks.com
email: Allison@AllisonSpeaks.com
or call 800-664-7641.

UPSIDE EVENTS AND EDUCATION

We want to hear your stories. Please join us on our blog at www.UpsideTheBook.com.

We offer year-round workshops, keynote lectures and retreats for individuals, employers, non-profit organizations and any other individuals or organizations interesting in developing in-depth strategies for sustainable success.

EMPLOYEE RESILIENCE PROGRAMS

- **Building Resilience during Turbulent Times** This series of half- to full-day workshops help employees cope with the stresses of current events and develop flexibility skills to handle the changes in their lives and the world, thereby liberating them to be more productive at work.

- **Managing during Turbulent Times** This unique series of workshops provides managers with the tools to supervise others without depleting their own productivity and reserves. Participants will learn to adapt and be more flexible when handling the common, day-to-day work-life conflicts that occur during economic or organizational changes.

Keynote Lectures

Thought provoking and inspirational, our 45- to 90-minute keynote lectures are highly customized to your organization or industry, encouraging adaptability and creative thinking to achieve sustainable success.

Retreats

Bring the whole family or your team to a weekend retreat for renewal.

FOR MORE INFORMATION CONTACT:

Allison Blankenship
Allison@MyOrganicSuccess.com
(205) 824-2004

Bonnie Michaels
mwfam@aol.com
(847) 308-0919
www.mwfam.com